UNCOMPROMISING
FAITH

UNCOMPROMISING FAITH

One Man's Notes
From Prison

PAVEL UHORSKAI
Translated by JAROSLAV VAJDA

PUBLISHING HOUSE

Copyright © 1992 Concordia Publishing House
3558 S. Jefferson Avenue, St. Louis, MO 63118–3968
Manufactured in the United States of America

Library of Congress Cataloging in Publication Data

Uhorskai, Pavel, 1919-
    Uncompromising faith: one man's notes from prison / Pavel Uhorskai; translated [from the Slovak] by Jaroslav Vajda.
    ISBN 0-570-04575-4
    1. Uhorskai, Pavel, 1919- . 2. Lutheran Church—Czechoslovakia—Clergy—Biography. 3. Prisoners—Czechoslovakia—Biography. 4. Persecution—Czechoslovakia—History—20th century. I. Title.
BX8080.U35A3 1992
284.1'092—dc20
[B]   92-12260
                                                                                              CIP

---

1 2 3 4 5 6 7 8 9 10   VP   01 00 99 98 97 96 95 94 93 92

Contents

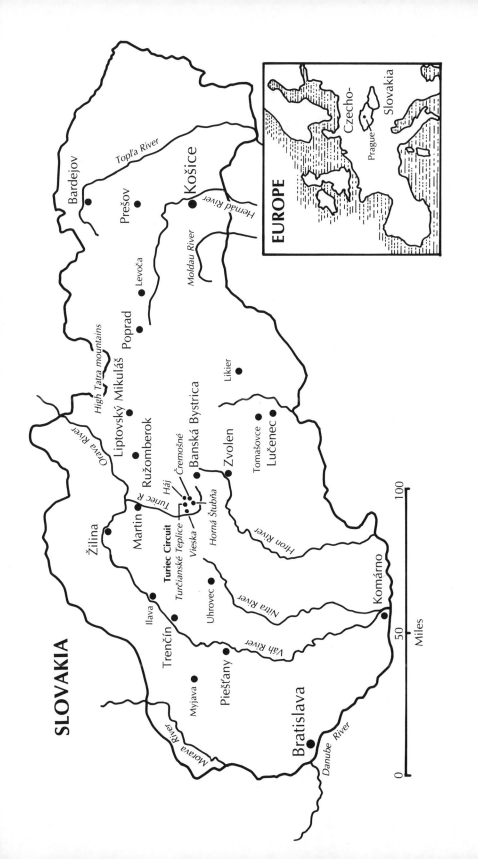

Geographical Pronunciation Guide

General Rules

Vowels:
>   a as in "father"
>   ä as in "bad"
>   e as in "bed"
>   i as in "pizza"
>   o as in "order"
>   u as in "duke"
>   y as in "duty"
>   j = y
>   á (accent acute lengthens the duration of the vowels)

Consonants:
>   ' following ď, ľ, and ť softens the consonant
>   č = tch as in "church"
>   ň = ny as in "news"
>   š = sh as in "she"
>   ž = zh as in "seizure"
>   c = ts
>   ch = kh, the German gutteral, as in Bach
>   w = v

Place Names

Banská Bystrica [BAHN–skah BEE–stree–tsah]
Banská Štiavnica [BAHN–skah SHTYAV–nee–tsah]
Bardejov [BAR–day–yov] (pop. 18,360)*
Batovce [BAH–tov–tseh]
Blatnice [BLAHT–nee–tseh]
Bojnice [BOY–ne–tsey]
Bratislava [BRA–tee–SLAH–vah]
Bratislava–Petržalka [PEH–tir–zhal–kah]
    (suburb of Bratislava; pop. 14,000)

Choč [KHOTCH]
Čierna Lehota [TCHYER–nah LEH–hoh–tah] (pop. 927)
Čremošné [TCHREH–mosh–neh] (pop. 219)
Dačov Lom [DAH–tchov LOM] (pop. 682)
Devičany [DEH–vee–TCHAH–nee]
Dolná Štubňa [DOL–nah SHTOOB–nyah] (pop. 500)
Dolný Kubín [DOL–nee KOO–bean] (pop. 10,219)
Háj [HIGH] (pop. 570)
Hanušovce nad Tepľou [HAH–noo–SHOV–tseh nad TEP–low]
   (pop. 2,219)
Hnúšťa [HNOOSH–tyah]
Horná Štubňa [HOR–nah SHTOOB–nyah] (pop. 2,156)
Hranice [HRA–nee–tseh]
Ilava [EE–lah–vah] (prison/former concentration camp)
Ivančina [EE–vahn–TCHEE–nah]
Jachymov [YAH–khee–mov] (German name: Joachimstal)
Kláštor [KLAHSH–tor]
Kokava [KO–ka–vah]
Komárno [ko–MAHR–noh]
Konventná Street [KON–vent–nah] Convent Street
Košice [KO–shee–tseh]
Koza Street [KO–zah] Goat Street
Kraskovo [KRAS–ko–voh] (pop. 232)
Krížna Street [KREEZH–nah] Street of the Cross
Leopoldov [LEH–oh–POL–dov] (penitentiary)
Levoča [LEH–vo–tchah]
Likier [LEE–kyer]
Limbach [a German name] (pop. 955)
Liptov [LEEP–tov]
Liptovská Porúbka [LEEP–tov–ska PO–roob–kah] (pop. 1,232)
Liptovský Mikuláš [LEEP–tov–skee MEE–koo–lahsh] (pop. 19,694)
Lovinobaňa [LO–vee–no–BAN–yah] (pop. 1,381)
Lučenec [LOO–tcheh–nets]
Ludrová [LOO–dro–vah] (pop. 1,097)
Luhačovice [LOO–ha–tcho–VEE–tseh]
Malé Stankovce [MA–leh STAN–kov–tseh] (pop. 276)

9

Martin [MAR–teen] (pop. 49,271)
Moldau River valley [MOL–dow]
Morava River [MO–ra–vah]
Myjava [MEE–yah–vah] (pop. 6,684)
Necpaly [NETS–pal–lee] (pop. 898)
Nové Mesto nad Váhom [NO–veh MES–toh nad VAH–hom]
Novohradský [NO–vo–hrad–skee]
Orava [O–rah–vah]
Ozdín [OZ–deen] (pop. 293)
Pankrác [PAHN–krats] (a prison)
Piešťany [PYESH–tya–nee]
Poltár [POL–tahr] (pop. 3,105)
Poprad [PO–prahd] (pop. 28,048)
Poprad–Stráž [PO–prahd STRAHZH] (a suburb of Poprad)
Prague [PRAHG]
Prešov [PRE–shov] (county seat; pop. 62,429)
Púchov [POO–khov] (pop. 9,946)
Rajec [RAH–yets] (pop. 5,123)
Rimavská Sobota [REE–mav–skah SO–bo–tah] (county seat; pop. 16,394)
Rožňava [ROZH–nya–vah] (pop. 83,843)
Ruská Street [ROOS–kah] Russian Street
Ružomberok [ROO–zhom–BEAR–ock] (pop. 23,435)
Sahy [SAH–hee]
Sedemchotare [SE–dem–kho–TAH–reh]
Sklené [SKLEH–neh] (pop. 1,353)
Sliač [SLEEATCH] (pop. 3,286)
Slovenské Pravno [SLO–ven–skeh PRAHV–noh] (pop. 1,020)
Sokolovo [SO–ko–LO–vo]
Spalená Street [SPAH–leh–nah] Burnt Street
Spiš County [SPEESH]
Spišska Nová Ves [SPEESH–ska NO–vah VES] (county seat; pop. 27,947)
Šafárikovo [SHA–fah–re–KO–voh]
Štrba [SHTIR–bah] (pop. 2,652)
Tomašovce [TO–mah–SHOV–tseh] (pop. 1,399)
Trenčín [TREN–tcheen] (county seat; pop. 40,307)
Trnava [TIR–nah–vah] (county seat; pop. 50,948)

Turany [TOO–rah–nee] (pop. 4,163)

Turčianské Teplice [TOOR–tchian–skeh TYEP–lee–tseh] (pop. 5,416)

Turiec [TOOR–yets]

Uhrovec [OO–hro–vets] (pop. 1,575)

Valdice [VAL–dee–tseh]

Veľká [VEL–kah] (pop. 1,527)

Vieska [VEES–kah] (pop. 196)

Vrbov [VIR–bov] (pop. 1,267)

Vrútky [VROOT–kee] (pop. 5774)

Vyšne Hágy [VEESH–neh HAH–gee]

Záhorie [ZAH–hor–yeh] (pop. 475)

Zvolen [ZVO–len] (county seat; pop. 30,680)

Žilina [ZHEE–lee–nah] (county seat; pop. 58,142)

* Most population figures are from the 1970 census.

Acronyms and Glossary

ČSM—Československý sväz mládeže (Czechoslovak Youth League)

DEM—Dorast evanjelickej mládeže (Junior Evangelical* Youth)

JEŽ—Jednota evanjelických žien (Union of Evangelical Women)

JRD—Jednotné roľnické družstvo (Union of Agricultural Workers)

MNV—Miestny národný výbor (Local National Committee)

NEM—Nedeľná (škola) evanjelickej mládeže
(Sunday School for Evangelical Youth)

NZ—Národné združenie (National Assembly)

ONV—Okresný národný výbor (District National Committee)

SECAV—Slovenská evanjelická cirkev augšburgského vierovyznania
(Slovak Evangelical Church of the Augsburg Confession)

SEM—Sdruženie evanjelickej mládeže (Association of Evangelical Youth)

SLOVÚC—Slovenský úrad (pre veci) cirkevné
(Slovak Office for Church Affairs)

SPEVAK—Spolok evangelických kňazov (Association of Evangelical Pastors)

SSM—Socialistický sväz mládeže (Socialist Youth League)

ŠTB—Štátna bezpečnosť (State Security/Secret Police)

UA—Učiteľská akadémia (Teachers Academy)

ÚAV/SNF—Ústredný akčný výbor Slovenského národného frontu
(Central Action Committee of the Slovak National Front)

ÚSEK—Ústredie slovenských evanjelických kňazov
(Coalition of Slovak Evangelical Pastors)

ZČSSP—Zväz Česko-Slovenského Sovietskeho priateľstva
(Czecho-Slovak/Soviet Friendship Union)

ZNB—Zbor národnej bezpečnosti (National Security/Police)

Akadémia—Academy/Junior College

Br.—"Brother," the familiar term for a fellow pastor

DE—A doctorate in engineering; thus, a title

Eng.—A university degree in engineering; thus, a title

Gymnázium—Preparatory school for college/university

Lýceum—Elementary and middle school

MD—A doctorate in medicine; thus, a title

* For "Evangelical" read "Lutheran"

12

Foreword

Historical Background

The Slovak people comprise one nation in the family of Slavs in Central and Eastern Europe [from Bohemia eastward to Russia and from Poland southward to Yugoslavia]. They have occupied the area of present-day Slovakia since the 6th to 7th centuries, and established their own state in the 9th century. Their Christianization dates back to the second half of the 9th century [A.D. 863].

The Lutheran Reformation came to Slovakia by the year 1521 and spread rapidly throughout the territory. By the end of the 16th century, 90 percent of the population of Slovakia was Protestant, overwhelmingly Lutheran.

In the second half of the 17th century, the Protestant population became the objects and victims of the Counter-Reformation, suffering discrimination, forced conversion, persecution, massacres, enslavement, and banishment. This situation lasted until the end of the 19th century, and finally moderated considerably after World War I.

Politically, the Slovak people (Catholic and Protestant) were threatened with total Magyarization and near-genocide by their Hungarian neighbors and overlords. After centuries of oppression, they achieved political freedom in 1918 in the Czecho-Slovak Republic. In the following two decades the Slovak people experienced tremendous cultural and spiritual growth. From 1939 to 1945 they came under Fascist domination, followed by a new liberation in 1945.

The year 1948 saw the communist coup d'etat, the establishment of atheism as the official "religion," and the persecution of the church and believers of every communion.

From that period comes this account of one Christian who survived to tell how it was: Bishop General Pavel Uhorskai.

Pavel Uhorskai was born March 2, 1919, in Tomašovce, Slovakia. Upon completing his studies in the *Gymnázium* and the Lutheran School of Theology in Bratislava, and following his five-year chaplaincy and ordination, he served as pastor of the congregation and parish in Háj, in the Turiec circuit of the Slovak Evangelical Church of the Augsburg Confession (SECAV). There he conducted a successful home mission ministry among the youth, devoting the major portion of his time to religious instruction.

His popularity in the parish and district brought him into disfavor with the political regime that came into power after the Communist takeover in 1948, resulting eventually in his arrest March 14, 1951. He was sentenced to two years and ten months in prison plus an additional five-year loss of his civil rights. However, he was released by presidential amnesty May 9, 1953, after having served only a year-and-a-half in prison.

After his release, Uhorskai labored as a woodcutter and warehouse worker. He was rehabilitated in 1969, and in 1971 was cleared by the court of the charges for which he had been sentenced and imprisoned. However, his application for the restoration of his preaching license was denied. Not permitted to function as a pastor, he served the church in the position of cantor, and after 1983 as supervisor of church work in Tomašovce, which duties he performed until his election to the office of bishop general of SECAV.

In the interim between his release from prison and the granting of his preaching license, Uhorskai met with a number of pastors in a secret theological study group. In 1969, they set forth 41 theses outlining a program for the renewal of the church, only to have them rejected by the church administration. In 1971, together with Brother Otto Vizner [see Appendix C], Uhorskai requested a discussion with the leaders of the church regarding the state of the church, but that petition was denied also.

Uhorskai's rehabilitation and restoration to the pastoral ministry was completed shortly after the November 1989 peaceful revolution. A year later, in November 1990, Pavel Uhorskai was festively installed as the bishop general of the Slovak Evangelical Church of the Augsburg Confession in the Czech and Slovak Federal Republic.

Preface

Remember those earlier days after you had received the light, when you stood your ground in a great contest in the face of suffering. Sometimes you were publicly exposed to insult and persecution; at other times you stood side by side with those who were so treated. You sympathized with those in prison and joyfully accepted the confiscation of your property, because you knew that you yourselves had better and lasting possessions.

Hebrews 10:32–34

Before I begin to tell how it was, let me remind the reader that this will not be an academic or fictitious account. This will be a record of actual events I witnessed, experienced, and endured to their conclusion. I do not wish to embellish anything nor make the situation seem worse than it was. Rather, I will be presenting from my point of view events that confronted not only me but the entire church. I shall note my own and the church's reaction to them. These pages will present an analysis of life in my time, of which my activity was a small excerpt, in order to explain how and why it happened that honorable and dedicated church workers were declared outlaws, thus being deprived of respect and of the possibility of serving the church.

1

The Path to Ministry

When I decided to study theology and prepare for the ministry, the clergy enjoyed a high level of respect, because of the important place the church occupied in society. Regrettably, the elevated position of the church was due not to its religious worth but chiefly to its value to society. The disastrous legacy of Constantine—the alliance of church and state—became rooted in Roman Catholicism long ago. And the Reformation, though it saw its essence in the Word of God and life in conformity to it, nevertheless failed to stop the Constantinian influence on the church. Church leaders and their followers secularized the church internally and externally, contrary to the Lord's exhortation not to be conformed to the world.

In the Slovak Evangelical Church of the Augsburg Confession (SECAV), the clergy continued their age-old national and political resistance to the Magyarization of Slovaks by the Hungarian and Austro-Hungarian government. The same pressure existed even in the Slovak Lutheran church in Hungary. In the course of time, certain Magyarized individuals denied their Slovak origin in favor of social or political careers. The same was true of pastors, who, though conscious of their Slovak nationality, pursued their professional and personal goals in social and political terms, while their commitment to the Gospel receded farther and farther into the background, gradually ending in dead formalism. They preferred to be masters rather than servants, despite the Lord's injunction to his followers, "Whoever wants to become great among you must be your servant, and whoever wants to be first must be slave of all" (Mark 10:43–44).

In coming to a decision about the pastoral ministry, I had no clear concept of an "inner call" and only a very confused idea of an "external call." Instead, the clearer concept of ministry was one of service, service to my Slovak people, more in the nationalist sense of Ľudovít Štúr's ideals than those of the Gospel. For this kind of

17

service, I saw the best potential in the pastoral ministry.

For this reason, I made a decision to study theology seriously, and I applied myself to it earnestly. My God-given intellectual and moral capacities enabled me to do this very well. Studies and examinations gave me no problems. I was able to resolve most academic questions by reading extensively in specialized and classical literature, an ability reflected in my historical dissertation, "Church History in Slovak Literature."

Not having to struggle with exams, I was able to devote time and energy to home mission activity. I participated in every organization accessible to me, from the Association of Evangelical Youth (SEM) to the Union of University Students. But dearest to me and the most time-consuming was my Sunday school work. In order to acquire greater knowledge in that field, I wished to go to Germany for my third undergraduate year (1940–41), but because of the war and at the advice of Dr. L. Jamnický, this was not realized.

I completed my studies at the School of Theology in Bratislava with a Th.B. degree. I was ordained, and my first position was as assistant chaplain to Dr. Ľudovít Žarnovicky in Uhrovec. The idea of "service according to the Gospel" became even more clarified for me by my seminary studies and by my youth ministry experience, and found its concrete expression in youth mission ministry.

To equip myself for such service, I endeavored to know everything that young people know or want to know, and then to place all that knowledge and my entire person into the service of our Lord Jesus Christ by becoming acquainted with him and following him privately and publicly, not only within the confines of the SECAV but beyond.

This was the work that occupied me from the very beginning as chaplain in all of the stations beyond Uhrovec: in Bardejov Štrba, Veľká, Poprad, Ružomberok, Martin, and Háj. My aim was to become proficient in my calling by working with SEM on committees of the national and regional youth organizations, and by taking various training courses.

During this period, I made another attempt to study abroad, but that came to naught, too.

Here I must note that already at the seminary and in parish life, a different wind was blowing than in previous generations. The political and social aspects of pastoring were retreating into the background and a spiritual dimension was moving to the fore. Seeking and asserting Christ's spirit in the world, in humanity, in the individual, and in oneself was becoming a priority. Various religious trends were being evaluated: orthodoxy, pietism, confessionalism, among others. Also being reexamined were the natural sciences, technology, and general scientific developments. We were coming to the conclusion that technical progress was not being matched by spiritual and moral progress.

Making the spiritual mission of the church our primary aim, we young chaplains were more interested in the internal condition of the church than in political issues. We criticized and rejected political influences in the church as well as the political abuse of the church. We wanted to serve the church as effectively as possible by further theological study, by evaluating current church programs, and by promoting all kinds of spiritually-motivated activities within the church.

During my chaplaincy, I prepared extensive studies on such subjects as "The Church and the Kingdom of God" and "Politics in Christianity." A number of us organized homiletical study groups in our pastoral conferences and exchanged sermonic studies. However, only about one-fourth to one-third of the pastors participated in analyzing the state of the church and in the drawing of a spiritual and moral profile of its members.

We also organized mission societies and conducted evangelization programs in all the congregations and preaching stations in the Turiec region, with great participation by the lay members and, I believe, with great success. I threw myself into the work deliberately and with fervent enthusiasm and genuine love. My concern was only for the church and the spiritual welfare of its people.

In addition to my activity in the Turiec region, I performed an evangelistic ministry in Dolný Kubín, Liptovský Mikuláš, Poprad–Stráž, and elsewhere. It should be noted that all these activities were approved and supported by the SECAV. But again, not all pastors participated in the program.

Reactions to our work were both favorable and unfavorable. I consider as favorable the fact that both church and unchurched people examined their private and public lives, and appreciated their new or renewed spiritual and moral direction.

I consider as unfavorable the fact that some people praised the evangelists instead of making changes in their own spiritual lives. Rather than applying the sermons to themselves for their good, they turned the message against others with whom they disagreed or considered worse than they. Among the "worse ones" they included Communists. Their unnecessary adulation of me gave me a good name among members of the church and a conspicuous name among enemies of the church, who then scrutinized my every step and examined my every act under a microscope, and judged the church and me in an unfriendly way.

2
A Fruitful
Pastoral Interlude

In 1946 I served as congregational chaplain in Martin [formerly St. Martin], the famous Slovak cultural center where the Lutheran church was strongly represented. The Martin church had a large membership and was prominent and respected in the community, though more for its cultural contributions than for its well-deserved spiritual influence.

The Martin congregation owned some fair church properties: a modest sanctuary and a new and spacious combination parsonage, office, meeting room, and fellowship hall. I became part of a well-run parish program and enjoyed a successful ministry while there. I taught in the local school and trade school and occasionally represented the principal, Dr. L. Vajdička, at the Štefánik Institute. I led the Association of Evangelical Youth (SEM) division, while Brother Vizner was in charge of the student section.

After the departure of the mostly Roman Catholic Germans from Horná Štubňa in 1946, and after the repatriation of Slovaks from Hungary and Bulgaria, there were left in the town, including the poorer inhabitants from the Turiec region, more than 550 Lutherans.

These parishioners were served by Pastor Šolc, who was getting ready to retire. I arrived there in 1946 to assist in organizing divine and prayer services, and so got to visit the parish regularly.

Then, at the beginning of 1947, a vacancy occurred in the congregation in Háj. I still did not want to be a full-time pastor of a church, because I kept hoping I would get to study abroad. But that opportunity continued to elude me, due to the conditions following World War II.

A number of candidates applied for the position in Háj, but none from the Turiec circuit. The older pastors pointed this out at the pastoral conferences, and Dean Holly reproached me for not applying to serve a congregation with my five-year experience as a chaplain, and my having completed my ministerial studies and passing my tutorial exams already in 1945. I was persuaded to at least submit a formal application in order to uphold the circuit administration's honor. I submitted the application as requested.

After preaching a sample sermon, I was unanimously elected pastor of the Háj parish. My pastorate began July 1, 1947, and I preached my first sermon as pastor there on July 6. The congregation welcomed me joyfully and with some fanfare in a beautiful installation service on September 28, 1947.

At that time the entire parish numbered some 2,500 souls. The mother church counted almost 500 souls, the remainder scattered throughout the preaching and teaching stations in Čremošné, Turčianské Teplice, Vieska, Dolná Štubňa (having the largest number of members), and Sklené.

The large number of young people in the Turčianské Teplice school and those in other local schools called for a special emphasis on a youth ministry. Having accumulated considerable experience in preaching and evangelizing as a chaplain, I decided to devote all my energy to mission work among the youth of the parish.

In four of the stations in the parish I held weekly meetings of two youth organizations. In Sklené, a third group met less frequently. If one were to add to those meetings 38 hours of religion classes I taught by myself every week, the handling of the mission program throughout the Turiec region, plus a large demanding parish with special functions (baptisms, weddings, funerals, confirmation instruction), various religious festivals, and assorted private consultations—one can see how busy I was. The only time left for study was late in the evening and during the night.

(Like the other pastors in the church, I sent a detailed account of my activities to the statistician at the church headquarters, who in turn passed it on to the district bishop's office in Liptovský Mikuláš. One can still find my pastoral records on file there.)

The facilities for religious instruction in the scattered parish were far from adequate. There were church schools only in Háj, Dolná Štubňa, and Čremošné. Elsewhere there were only public schools. Prior to 1948, we conducted worship services and various meetings also in public schools. But after 1948 we were banned from them as well as from former church schools. When public or church schools were no longer open to us, we met in the homes of church members. That alternative turned out to be a happy recourse and a blessed one. And that instruction proved to be the most beautiful of all.

However, despite my best intentions, efforts, abilities, and good health, I could not keep up with the work. It was necessary to find and train assistants. In a short time I had more than 50 at my disposal. The volunteer staff was made up of students, teachers, officials, presbyters, and trustees. The more we worked together, the more joy we derived from our combined efforts. As a result, I had the entire parish in my hand, as it were. I lived in Háj. As often as four times a week I visited Turčianské Teplice and Vieska; Dolná Štubňa at least once a week. Every other week I visited Horná Štubňa and Sklené, and Čremošné once a month. My members knew where to find me at any hour when I was not at the parsonage. And how they found me! I must say we had a true family relationship.

At first I walked to all my classes and meetings in Turčianské Teplice and Dolná Štubňa. Later I acquired a bicycle, which I used to get to Bible classes—often in bad weather and late at night. When my parishioners saw how tiring that was, they offered to transport me to all the Bible classes by horse and buggy in the summer and by a horse-drawn sleigh in the winter. What a delight to have such a favor offered without any complaint or request on my part, purely of their own initiative!

It was my practice to take two or three of my parishioners, young and old, with me to various church affairs in other congregations. And in my home congregation I prepared prayer and mission weeks, during which two speakers made presentations every day. One such evening with our church workers in Sweden left an exceptionally profound impression on those present.

I also arranged religious conferences with the religion classes I conducted at the local *Akadémia* and *Gymnázium*. The sessions lasted two or three days and concluded with the celebration of the Lord's Supper. Preparations for the conference were made two months in advance, with a theme chosen by the class members. I gathered the materials, divided them among the student participants, and served as the director of the entire program. The students enjoyed and benefited from the conference, reports of which appeared in the church periodical *The Evangelical Messenger from the Tatra Foothills* (*Ev. posol z pod Tatier*).

In addition, I organized student outings to Choč and Liptov, where young people from the surrounding regions of Turiec, Orava, and Liptov assembled in a Lutheran spirit. I am grateful to Supervisor Čaplovič for arranging a rail discount for these outings and for, afterwards, officially accepting and filing my account of the events. My work with young people was gratifyingly successful with what I believe was the blessing of the Lord Jesus. I enjoyed the maximum trust of my parishioners and of the youth in particular. I could turn to them with confidence for whatever help I needed. They did what they could out of love for their church and their pastor. Never before had they led as active and intensive a spiritual life as they did then.

3

The Nightfall of Atheistic Communism

Then came the year 1948—and the Communist takeover of the government. The party assumed total control, and despite its wily subterfuges regarding religious freedom, it set out to replace religion with Marxist-Leninism, hesitatingly at first, then gradually more boldly and ruthlessly.

The Communist party had always regarded religion as the opiate of the masses. (See Pavlikov's *The Development of Soviet Education and Pedagogy*, which stresses that one cannot be content with private atheism; everyone must become an aggressive atheist and join the campaign to wipe out religion completely.) The Party has never concealed or denied this philosophy. It simply does not publicize it, but acts according to it as far as circumstances permit.

The Catholic Action program that operated in our country at the time serves as a typical example of the Party's methods. The alleged aim of the program was to separate the Roman Catholic church from the papacy and from the Vatican and to give it an independent, national character. Actually, the plan was intended to liquidate the church altogether. All kinds of programs were created to persuade or force people to join the movement. The proponents enlisted anyone they could to carry out their plan: Catholics, non-Catholics, and atheists.

And so it was that the director of the District National Committee (ONV), Mr. Obuch, approached me in order to enlist me in the Catholic Action movement. I rejected the appeal categorically, stating I had nothing to do with the program, nor did I wish to, besides being a Lutheran pastor. To which he replied that as a Lutheran I have the same negative attitude toward the Pope and the Roman Catholic church, and I should therefore join the program.

I rejected his argument out of hand, saying, "I do indeed disagree with the papacy and the Roman Catholic church, but for different reasons from yours. Mine are theological and biblical. Your reasons are political and atheistic. And as such they are unacceptable to me. Today you are openly fighting the Roman Catholic church, and your so-called 'Catholic Action' is simply another evidence of your hostility being directed against the strongest church in our land. But this fight your party is waging will come around to us [Lutherans] also, although we are less important to you politically and economically. Eventually we will meet on the battlefield as adversaries, but I will oppose you for spiritual and ideological reasons. And that will be no less fierce a battle."

He then changed the subject. We talked about the social character of the church, the revolutionary changes in society with the advent of Christianity, and about Christian socialism. I quoted the incident of Ananias and Sapphira, which he didn't seem to know. Strange, for he had been a Lutheran originally, and I had given his granddaughter Tanya religious instruction. I must say, however, that he did not behave aggressively toward me.

On another front a massive membership campaign was launched by and for the Czecho–Slovak/Soviet Friendship Union (ZČSSP). In Háj it was conducted by a member of the National Security/Police (ZNB) and a member of the Local National Committee (MNV), a certain Blanka Bakošova, a Lutheran who had previously been president of a branch of the Union of Evangelical Women (JEŽ). They, too, visited me with a polite request to join the ZČSSP.

In turn I asked them how such membership would benefit me. Would it enable me to further my theological studies? Would the Union provide me with specialized literature? Would it provide me with contacts with the Eastern Orthodox and other church bodies in the USSR?

They answered, "No, it would not."

"Well then," I concluded, "I cannot and do not wish to join you, for the Union has no meaning for me."

Additional pressure was applied to me personally to become involved in the Union of Agricultural Workers (JRD), since the ONV knew of my popularity among my parishioners, most of whom were farm workers, how they trusted me, and the respect I enjoyed in the community.

"I have no objection to the JRD," I replied, "but that is not my responsibility. Let the paid workers of the ONV recruit members for the organization, not I. I have no experience in this area, and besides, I don't own a furrow of land. How would it look if I, a landless person who doesn't own a furrow and who will not work in the fields or in any agricultural job, were to recruit people to join the JRD? We know the JRD is having a difficult time. People are earning little enough for themselves, and they are asked to turn over everything to the JRD. They would have every reason to point to me and say that I am doing well and that it is easy for me to persuade them to join the JRD, since I have no investment in it, nor would I have to depend on it for my income. They could say I have other income and would have everything to gain and nothing to lose by joining the Union. This could only harm my pastoral work. Therefore I cannot be a recruiter for your Union."

The officials of the ONV in Turčianské Teplice tried hard to win me over to their organization. I steadfastly rejected their campaign, stating my reasons from the Bible and the constitution and practice of the church. Turčianské Teplice being such a small town, I could not avoid meeting people and getting involved in frequent debates with otherwise friendly townsfolk.

After February 1948, quite some time elapsed before the government decided to deal with the Lutheran and Roman Catholic clergy. The first conference including all clergy from the Turiec region was called for April 29, 1949, in Martin, and was conducted by School Inspector Ondrejček, the cultural reporter of the ONV. In his presentation he urged us to trust and cooperate with the government agency and invited us to discuss the matter.

In the first such discussion, the Roman Catholic clergy were treated very carefully. With flattery and all kinds of strokes, the officials behaved like a cat around a dish of hot pudding. Zanyi, speaking for the Eastern Orthodox clergy, stated more to the point that cooperation with the ONV would be much simpler if the Communist party abandoned its materialistic worldview, a condition repeated even more critically by Prof. Ďurica from Kláštor.

No one rose to speak on behalf of our Lutheran church, not even Dean Hollý or the president of the pastoral conference, Horváth, or Vajdička from Martin. So I volunteered to speak.

I appealed for sincerity and truth in the relations between government agencies and the church, without hidden or ulterior motives. I spelled out the following unacceptable actions of the state toward the church.

1. Members of the ONV appearing on Sunday mornings to send churchgoers out on work brigades.

2. Interference in community affairs. Heretofore it was customary to elect the most-respected citizens to official posts. Now those officials were removed from office and replaced by people of defective character. For example, in Dolná Štubňa, a man from Háj who had deserted his wife and seven children and was living with another woman in an illicit relationship was appointed president of the local branch of the ONV.

3. The ONV issuing a notice that any employer of more than three workers was expected to take part in a demonstration and welcome for Commissioner L. Novomeský's visit to Martin. That went against my Lutheran conscience.

I spoke for three-quarters of an hour, listing all the irregularities taking place in public affairs and in the attitudes toward the church. I also mentioned the impact of these developments on church work then and in the future. My remarks were greeted with enthusiastic applause, and the meeting was abruptly concluded without further debate.

I left there about half an hour later and headed for Trenčín to a conference of Lutheran pastors from the entire Czechoslovak Republic. When I boarded the train in Martin, my fellow passengers discussed my comments. There was a strong reaction to them among the Catholics and political activists. In Trenčín I informed Dean Šenšel about the meeting.

In September 1948, our church office received from the government commission in Bratislava the proposed regulation concerning the economic security of the church by the state. We were to become familiar with it, study it, and report our reactions to it with our comments. From the church headquarters we were sent direct orders to take a stand on the new statute at our congregational meetings. This we did not do.

I don't think the church officials knew what to do with the situation. I myself felt helpless in the face of this pressure from the government, and I didn't care to respond at all. Later I came to the conclusion that the proposal would become law without the church's or my approval. But since I was sure that I would some day blame myself for not taking a personal stand on the matter, I drew up my report and comments regarding the proposed ordinance on October 13, 1948. It was a negative report, a copy of which I still have in my possession [Appendix A.] I don't know if all the pastors responded in such detail to the proposed statute. Apart from mine, the other reports from the Turiec circuit were quite general, neither salty nor greasy.

The government worked hard to prepare a foundation for the proposed law and authorized emissaries from the National Assembly (NZ) to interview Lutheran pastors in the various circuits of the church in order to bring concrete reports to the government. I don't know how they proceeded with the Catholics. Our [Lutheran] meeting was to be conducted by Vladimír Čaplovič, Communist party delegate and former director of the *Gymnázium,* and by Andrej Žiak, a delegate from the Slovak Progressive Party and General Presbyter of the Lutheran church.

The convocation of the Turiec circuit was called for (the town of) Martin on August 27, 1949, at 6 P.M. in the church meeting hall.

Žiak began the meeting with a "very important" introduction. "I have been authorized by the Czechoslovak government to call this meeting. I want to speak to you as the General Presbyter of the SECAV, as one who desires only the welfare of the church, and for that reason I want to talk to you about the proposed law."

He then spoke in general terms about the church-state situation in our Lutheran church, about the situation as it applies to the Roman Catholic church, about the dissolution of the churches, and the supreme authority of the state. The church had three choices in regard to the state: (1) open hostility, (2) complete isolation, or (3) mutual support and respect. The state, he said, was involving itself in church teachings. Some kind of modus vivendi was necessary. Furthermore, one had to remember the many forces the [Lutheran] church had had to face in the past. The "Away from Rome" movement had failed. During the Slovak State (1939–45) the Lutheran charter was not recognized, there was an unfavorable school law, and so on.

He went on to explain that in the current relationship with the state, the Roman Catholic church was compromised by the previous era, by its dependence on the Vatican, by its size as the largest church body in the country, and by its wealth in church properties. The new statute, he implied, was aimed at the Catholic church and not at our Lutheran church.

Of the Lutheran church, Čaplovič said, "I see the Lutheran church as progressive, and I do not see the proposed statute as hampering our progress. The Czechoslovaks, the Unitarians, the Greek Orthodox, and the Bohemian Brethren all agree with the proposal. The difference in the proposal is the omission of the phrase 'without confession.' Everything else remains: the right to receive [and the members' right to give] honoraria, as well as the church's right to manage its daily affairs. The church tax is abolished. And, oh yes, the church must not condemn the Marxist ideology of dialectical materialism . . ."

Čaplovič spoke at some length. A discussion followed, neither salty nor greasy. Five or six pastors took a stand in favor of the ordinance, one of whom was Viktor Schimko.

He said, "It will be better for us than it has ever been. In a sense, pastors will be officials of the government, supported by the authority of the state. They won't have to bother with New Year's collections or depend on honoraria. They will be held in high regard."

Other pastors took a moderately negative position toward the proposal.

I then asked to say a few words. I referred to my written report of October 13, 1948, which I had sent to the ÚAV/SNF (the Central Action Committee of the Slovak National Front). Then I pointed to Schimko's report about the Eastern Orthodox church in the USSR. It revealed that the number of religious books published by the largest church body in the USSR was smaller in quantity and variety than that of the SECAV. If our prospects were to be compared with those of the Eastern Orthodox, what kind of limitations would we be facing in Czechoslovakia?

"You say that you believe this law will be only to our benefit," I continued, "that it will produce greater growth? I can, however, repeat a statement by a Communist party delegate who said of this proposed regulation: 'The church will either accept the proposed statute and thereby sign its own death warrant and eventually perish; or it will resist and be dealt a blow to the head. One way or the other it will perish.' This law is intended for the liquidation of the church."

At this point, Žiak interrupted me very solemnly and said, "Reverend Pastor, these are very serious words. Are you willing to repeat them, because I will have to make them known at the proper time."

I replied, "Yes, and I can tell you who said them. It was Director Vladimir Čaplovič in the *Gymnázium* dining hall in Turčianské Teplice." I then repeated the quote slowly so he could write it down word for word.

And so the meeting ended, with Žiak taking with him the negative reaction of the Turiec circuit. In an article in *Church Letters* [*CL*], the official organ of SECAV, he published an article in which he said he "believed" the laws would prove a blessing for SECAV, that he "was convinced the government had only the welfare of the church in mind" (*CL*, 1949, pp. 330–346).

The Lutheran constituency, however, had no such position or impression, particularly the Lutheran pastors who rejected the proposed statute in a memorandum entitled "The Piešťany Manifesto" (Appendix B), issued at the general pastoral conference in Piešťany on September 23, 1949, a conference attended by 172 pastors and 34 pastors' wives.

The Piešťany Manifesto expresses the negative position of the Lutheran pastors jointly and individually toward the statute itself as well as to the very idea of such a law. Immediately after the sessions, the officers of the Association of Evangelical [Lutheran] Pastors (SPEVAK) sent their declaration to all political forums, to all members of the National Assembly, to all institutions, and to all national leaders. In addition, this formal reaction to the proposal was received by Čepička, the already-functioning Minister for the Slovak Office for Church Affairs (SLOVÚC).

It is said that the very evening Čepička received the report, he heard a Western foreign radio broadcast quoting the very manifesto. This so agitated him that he immediately summoned the representatives of the Lutheran church to Prague to take them to task for their action. I think the delegation included Dr. Adamiš, F. Ruppeldt, and Eng. Zatko. Žiak told me on January 19, 1950, that when the delegation arrived in Prague, Čepička was on the verge of madness and coarsely berated the Lutheran representatives for rejecting the proposed ordinance.

This is what Čepička said, word for word: "The Catholic clergy are our enemies, but what they are doing is at least tactful and proper. But what you Slovak Lutherans are doing is neither tactful nor proper."

In the meeting he shouted insults at the church delegates as if they were street urchins. The delegates were so shocked that they were unable to respond. Žiak felt sorry for the way the delegates were treated and defended them.

"Honorable Sir," Žiak said, "the restrained position of the Lutheran church is both justified and understandable. For at one of the conferences dealing with the proposed ordinance, which I was authorized to convene, I verified a statement made about the proposal." And here he quoted my words from the Martin consultation: "The church will either accept the proposed law and so write its own death warrant and slowly perish—or it will resist and be dealt a death blow. Either way, it will be done for!"

The statement again riled Čepička. All he could bring himself to say, in Czech, was, "Who said that?!"

Žiak replied, "I can't tell you who said it, but I verified it at the conference."

And with that the hearing ended, and the church representatives were dismissed without any sanctions.

Then Žiak said to me, "Reverend Sir, if you had done nothing for the church but this, if only for the fact that the SECAV delegates could leave that hearing without loss, you deserve acknowledgment and thanks. But now it will be necessary to prove who made the statement."

I assured him it was a simple matter. "Let's go to the academy in Turčianské Teplice, and we'll confirm it on the spot."

I cleared off my desk, which was covered with my preparations for our annual congregational meeting, and asked him to drive me to the school. When we arrived at the building, Žiak, evidently afraid, didn't want to go in with me.

When I entered the building, I asked the professors in the meeting room if they remembered when Director Čaplovič made the statement about the proposed ordinance. They all said, "Yes, yes, we know." and recalled some other details as well.

However, when I explained to them that what was now needed was for the statement to be confirmed, one after the other said, "Leave me out of it! I don't want anything to do with it. You know how inconsiderate and arrogant Čaplovič is."

I went out to Žiak in his car and told him what was said. However, since it was Wednesday and no religion classes were scheduled, I told Žiak I would try to get the Catholic catechete Hríbik's testimony. When I got hold of Hríbik the next day, he dodged the question, saying, "Yes, but couldn't you rephrase the remark more mildly?"

I sneered and said this was not a matter of style but of fact.

In the end, Director Vladimir Čaplovič proved to be the most courageous of all. When he was confronted by the Communist party about whether or not he had made the statement, he said, "If Pastor Uhorskai claims I said it, then I said it."

With that the case was closed. Of course, somewhat later, Čaplovič was not elected a delegate of the Communist party. My guilt for the statement was erased. But my courage in quoting it and challenging the government authority did not go unnoticed. I became a hounded suspect.

I think this was the beginning of my road to prison.

4

What Got Me Arrested

As I said before, from my student days I devoted myself zealously to mission activity. Our church's home mission department provided at least three mission centers for youth. I had heard of them, but had not attended any of them. I was invited to lead two sessions, one in August of 1948 and a second in July of 1949, presenting workshops for older working youth and post-high school students, training them for leadership roles.

I strove to give the centers a valuable religious substance with honesty and sincerity. Without going into the details of the courses, I had two impressions of the attending students. There were those who were genuinely interested in leading a religious life, and there were those who just wanted to spend a pleasant vacation.

Regrettably, there were two students who had no apparent interest in religion but seemed to be there to sabotage the program. They were a young man by the name of Takáč and a girl named Hela Hájniková, whose father worked in the bishop's office in Bratislava. Takáč flaunted his contempt for religion openly, considering it reactionary and hypocritical, and shouting in his more candid moments, "Hang the reactionaries!" Hájniková apologized for him and defended him when I called him on his behavior.

I ran into Hájniková again in 1953 upon my release from prison. At that time she was the head nurse in a tuberculosis sanitarium in Vyšne Hágy under her married name, Najchráková. In a letter to me she offered to help me find employment, but on the condition that I give up my religious convictions. Only after years in prison and forced labor was I able to see how atheism had systematically tried to penetrate every aspect of life, including religion.

In the following year, 1950, the state had already confiscated the mission centers of the church, forbade such activity, and replaced them with international Pioneer Youth camps.

My congregation took a selfish attitude toward my work in the mission center, saying that I was the pastor of the Háj parish and should restrict my duties to it. However, since I had the approval of the church administration for my mission activity, they did not make an issue of it. Eventually they came to the conclusion that the congregation also benefited from their pastor's mission activity outside the local church. I regarded my work at the mission center a blessing, and was and am thankful for it.

My home mission work was a blessing to me as well, as I conducted the programs of the various Lutheran youth groups. The greatest difficulty was finding places to hold meetings. After 1948 we were not allowed to use the public school facilities. Even though some school authorities closed their eyes to the use of their space, the schools began to be inconvenient.

As attendance at the Association of Evangelical Youth (SEM) meetings began to fall off, I decided to abandon the school premises and meet with the young people in private homes. This proved to be a propitious step. Both parents and children liked the arrangement, and it enabled me to get families involved in their children's religious training. Families vied with one another to host the classes, considering it an honor and a privilege. And I, as their pastor, had the unique opportunity to become acquainted with the problems, worries, and joys of each family. For the church, the arrangement proved to serve as a revival of its spiritual life.

This tactic, of course, prompted a negative reaction among those who wanted to destroy the church and the religious life of its people. They labeled this activity "an illegal gathering of young people," especially since the SEM had been outlawed.

I was visited personally by K. Kirsteuer, the president of the local Slovak National Front. He didn't mince words. "Pastor, a charge has been filed against you for illegally assembling young people. I rejected the charge at the district office as untrue. I said you weren't doing this. So I'm asking you to stop it."

That warning came from a former church teacher and believer, who at first used to attend our gatherings with his wife. I could see he wanted to help me in his way. I explained that I was doing nothing in secret, that the meetings were public and a part of my pastoral duties. He understood my position, but he did not fail to remind me that he had warned me against possible danger. It wasn't his concern alone, he said. The entire District National Committee was aware of it.

Those officials were obviously ambivalent and indecisive. They seemed to have succumbed to the satanic lure, "I will give you all this, if only you will fall down before me." Subsequently many others joined their ranks, including avowed enemies of the church, not realizing whose spirit was controlling them.

It was legally impossible to forbid me openly to do mission work as a pastor. And as I did not permit myself to be intimidated, it became necessary to find some allegation that would become an obstacle to my work.

The allegation was found: "You are against the Socialist Youth League (SSM)."

At the *Gymnázium* and in the *Akadémia,* there was a strong political (actually, Communistic) indoctrination of the youth. Under the cloak of this program the youth could do anything. For example, they went as cultural shock troops in the JRD to organize new SSMs in the villages. Of course, this activity lasted into the late night hours. Sometimes they didn't get home until dawn. Their parents complained to me about a situation that I couldn't help noticing in school. I admonished the students to get back on the right track. The guilty ones reported my correction of them to the officers of the ONV, with the result that I was accused of being against the SSM. I had a hard time proving what I was really opposed to.

The political administrator of the school used this accusation to forbid my volunteer assistants from attending SEM Bible and religious training classes. He said, "I cannot permit attendance of the students in the Lutheran youth meetings, because the school would be responsible if they had an accident on the way to or from the classes."

My attempts to reason with him failed. I was no longer given any assistants from the school, from the boarding school in particular. This prohibition effectively stifled my program with the Lutheran youth organizations.

5

How the Church Lost
Its Independence

At the end of 1949—October 14, to be exact—the National Assembly passed the law establishing control of the [Lutheran] church by the state. It was enacted even though the church had not approved it. This was evident from the spontaneous and unambiguous declaration of the Association of Evangelical Pastors (SPEVAK) in Piešťany in the Piešťany Manifesto. Only a handful of individuals tried every argument to postpone the conference's statement. On behalf of the laity it was Andrej Žiak, simultaneously delegate to the National Assembly and General Presbyter of the SECAV, a teacher/cantor in Nové Mesto nad Váhom, who was under the strongest political pressure to try every means to force the church to approve the law.

The law went into effect at the National Assembly's session as Statute #217. The law establishing the Slovak Office of Church Affairs (SLOVÚC) was passed the same day as #218, which established the control of the church by the state while assuring the church's economic security.

The pastors who were already in the service of the political activists did not dare pressure the overwhelming majority to approve the law. So when the law went into effect, it was necessary for the church to take a stand on it. A special general conference was called for that purpose in Bratislava October 25, 1949.

The conference vote was negative, even though the church leaders (Bishops Čobrda and Ruppeldt, and Dean Šenšel) were convinced that the motion had to be approved, because the law was already a fact, and not accepting it would place the church into an illegal situation. Nevertheless, Brother Lacko Adamčík from Devičany moved to reject the motion. In the end, the conference voted to send the government and commissioners a "Declaration" regarding the new relationship between the [Lutheran] church and the state.

The congregations of the church were apprised of the new laws, and a commission was set up to prepare a revised declaration for the following general conference scheduled for November 25, 1949. The declaration appeared in *Church Letters* (*Cirkevné Listy*) under the heading "Statute Concerning the Election of Pastors." In the meantime, the political authorities had received the church's formal approval of the law.

The decision to accept the statute was not reached freely. Decisions were made under pressure from the state. When I spoke to Bishop General Vladimir Čobrda a few days later and expressed my dismay over the church's stand, he replied, "What was I to do? Was I to turn over more than three hundred pastors' wives, and many times that number of children, to persecution? I could not take this upon my conscience."

I objected to the assumption that the pastors and bishops were unwilling to make a sacrifice for their faith, and said that this was the time for such a sacrifice to be made. I was unsuccessful in my objection, and so the church brought upon itself the heavy yoke described by Delegate Čaplovič.

The law went into effect, and we were obliged to live according to it. There were enough zealots to support it, who were less concerned about the church than about their careers and opportunities to curry favor with the state.

The church administration took specific steps to adjust to the new conditions. General Superintendent DE Peter Zatko wrote about them in *Church Letters* (1949, p. 379), saying: "We do not yet know how the state's agenda for the [Lutheran] church and its organizations will develop in the government's Office on Church Affairs (SLOVUK). The representative of this commission in Slovakia, Dr. Gustav Husák, assured us that, as it respects the interests of the state, the church can function essentially as in the past."

At the time, the church administrators did not suspect what lay behind the phrase "as it respects the interests of the state." They did not realize that this was the beginning of an open fight against religion. Soon thereafter the state began its first investigation of pastors prior to granting them a government license, without which it was impossible to conduct the pastoral office.

Beginning in July 1950, the presidium of the ONV summoned the pastors of all the churches to an inquiry. They were to appear collectively and in small groups. In my case they made an exception. I was not called with the others, but separately.

Those who were summoned collectively were given a speech about the right of the state to exercise supreme supervision over the churches, about the state's good intentions in caring for the church, about the financial security of the church and its pastors, that pastors are therefore employees of the state, and that consequently the state will oversee their activities and require of them an oath of allegiance.

The clergy were asked if they were ready to take such a loyalty oath. Without it, one could not receive a license to conduct the pastoral office. Thereupon pastors individually placed their oath of allegiance in the hands of the chairman of the ONV, had it recorded officially, and the matter was settled.

The loyalty oaths were made without publicity. I learned of them quite late after the ceremony took place, when some pastors asked me if I had already made my pledge.

After some ten days, the ONV called me in for a consultation without telling me why. We agreed on an afternoon appointment, when I would not be teaching at the school.

I expected the meeting would be informal and brief, as the others were. I should have known better.

Present were Ján Marčičiak, chairman of the ONV, Vice-Chairman Pavel Černák, Mihajľov, the cultural representative of the ONV, and I as the delinquent. We talked about the church in the past, during the National Uprising (1945) after the War, the socialization of the villages, the Communist takeover of Czechoslovakia in February 1948, the Union of Agricultural Workers (JRD), conditions within the church, activities of the church, and everything imaginable. We played the game for some four hours! I had no idea where it was headed.

Finally, and quite abruptly, the chairman told me to stand, and very formally asked me if I wished to pledge my allegiance to the republic. I answered that my allegiance was self-evident, that I had fought for the republic, that such a question surprised me, and that there could be no doubt as to my loyalty to the republic.

The chairman addressed me in an official tone of voice, repeated the question, and requested a direct reply.

I said, "I wish to." He and the other two men shook my hand, and the matter ended with my signature.

Then a more or less private debate ensued, in which he said with a smile that I was the biggest rebel in the district.

I countered with a smile and a question, "How can you call me a rebel since I haven't led any rebellion?"

"Well," he said, "the other pastors accept everything willingly and humbly, but you have a personal opinion about everything."

I retorted jokingly that I assumed we were living in a democratic republic, and we parted amicably.

I took note, however, of the watchfulness of the ONV officers, while retaining an outward calm and openness. They could sense my moral advantage over them. I suggested a public meeting with them in which they would present their case for socialism without religion and without the church, and I would talk about socialism with religion. We would debate publicly and see how they would defend their position and how the assembled audience would accept it.

They turned down my proposal as impossible, saying that I would have an advantage over them because I enjoyed the greater sympathy and favorable disposition of the populace.

We parted in good humor, and even though I wondered how they got the idea that I was the biggest rebel in the district—or who told them I was—I did not take it seriously.

6

Church Life
under Scrutiny

The law governing the economic security of the church was already binding. And the state began acting accordingly. Every congregation was obliged to present a budget. Many thought that the time had come when congregations would no longer have financial worries, because the state would assume them. (So thought the pastors à la Schimko.) And so they presented deficit budgets, requesting more than 50 percent subsidy from the state treasury. At the ONV, the financial committee thought the process a farce.

I presented my budget too, but asked for no subsidy for my parish. I had estimated the budget according to the means of our parish, thereby prompting ONV Chairman Marčičiak's comment: "Uhorskai doesn't want anything from this beggarly state."

I ignored his remark. But I was seriously convinced that congregations should depend entirely upon themselves for their church operation. Any supplemental support from the state would prove a "Danaan gift" [*Time Danaos et dona ferentes:* "Beware of Greeks bringing gifts"]. My congregation agreed with me.

The force of the new regulation was evident also in the fact that as early as 1950 our church was no longer permitted to operate any mission centers. Religion classes were held in all first- and second-level schools, that is, in public, middle, and technical schools. But there was a rumor afloat that a modification regarding religious instruction would soon be made.

I had been very consistent in the religion classes in the schools. The courses were not a mere pastime but required serious and intensive study. Students were given special assignments on various practical themes such as "Missions and religious propaganda vs. atheistic propaganda," "Prayers for various occasions," "How do I look at spiritual life?" "What do religion and the church mean to

41

me?" "Analyze hymns from the *Tranoscius* (the Slovak Lutheran hymnal) for content and meaning," and similar subjects. I assigned questions that would lead them into the Scriptures and derive a practical application of Biblical precepts for their life.

Many took the courses seriously and gladly. Others argued that these methods were not followed anywhere else. There were even some who publicized the courses to school principals and teachers, with the result that some instructors said they would like to attend my Bible classes themselves, and a few of them did indeed audit them.

At the time, it did not occur to me to interpret their attendance as anything other than a sincere interest in religion. Today I'm not too sure that another purpose was not at play. In any case, the anti-religious winds blowing through society only fanned my ardor for my calling.

The end of the 1949–50 school year had arrived. According to custom, I planned to gather the [Lutheran] students from the Háj, Dolná Štubňa, and Turčianské Teplice schools in our church for a closing service marking the end of the school year on June 28, 1950. I began my preparations with the students and school principals some seven days before the end of the term. All went well in every school except the one in Turčianské Teplice, where the principal, Pavel Černák, announced that he would not permit his students to attend a joint worship service with the other schools because it would disrupt their regular class schedule.

The true reason was different. When I pointed out that there was no regular schedule of classes on June 28, he merely shrugged and said nothing. Could it have been that his reasons were determined by the fact that he was also a vice-chairman of the ONV?

I said I would complain to the ONV that he was impeding the practice of religion for the students and myself. He told me to go ahead. So I went to the ONV office and asked to meet with its chairman, Ján Marčičiak. When I explained the problem, he told me encouragingly, "Don't worry; it can be done."

That was Friday, June 24. On Saturday I asked him to give me a definite reply. He made an excuse that he had not been able to arrange it, but that he would give me an answer by Sunday morning so that I could make an announcement in church. He made no arrangements and gave me no answer. So I was unable to make a public announcement of the service.

On Monday, June 27, I went to see Marčičiak personally at the ONV for a definite answer. He summoned the church secretary, Mihajľov, and Vice-Chairman Černák, the director of the town school who did not want to release his students, and we began conferring. Marčičiak pretended to have wanted to allow the church service, but implied that Černák was against it and had reported the matter to the Communist party office. Mihajľov was undecided. In the end, Černák's opinion prevailed, with the result that I was not allowed to hold the closing service.

At this I requested that they give me the decision in writing. They hedged and refused to do so. I insisted and, after a painful debate, they agreed to give me the written ban. But when it was written, there was no one willing to sign it. Again, after a tiresome hassle, they persuaded Mihajľov to sign it as the church secretary. He signed it, and I picked up the decree.

Having lost nearly two hours with this matter, I arrived late for my religion class with the third grade in the *Gymnázium,* where the students were waiting for me patiently. I apologized for the delay, and, after the regular opening of the period, I explained why I was late. I showed the students the decree with the signature and the seal of the ONV.

Understandably, I was somewhat agitated, but I managed to suppress my emotions. I told them something like this:

"Our government constitution guarantees freedom of religion, but when we want to go to church, they forbid us to hold a worship service. See, here is the decree of the ONV. From it we can see that the church is headed for difficult times. But this is not the first such instance in the history of the church.

"The struggle between faith and unbelief is as old as humanity itself, and was present already at the Fall in Paradise, at the Flood, in the entire history of God's chosen people, and at the appearance and death of Jesus Christ. The warfare between faith and unbelief has continued throughout the history of the church, in the death of multitudes of martyrs, and in the life and death of Master Ján Hus. It raged during the Reformation, then in the Lutheran Church, and it is going on to this very day. And yet we know that in this battle

God has never been defeated, and that the blood of martyrs is the seed of new confessors.

"This hostility is described in Psalm 2:1–4: 'Why do the nations conspire and the people plot in vain? The kings of the earth take their stand and the rulers gather together against the Lord and against his Anointed One. "Let us break their chains," they say, "and throw off their fetters." The One enthroned in heaven laughs; the Lord scoffs at them.'

"The battle has come to us, but it is futile against God. 'The moon isn't frightened when the dogs bark at it,' said Belo Klein-Tesnoskalský, quoted in his biography of Matthew Bahýl', when he addressed the persecutors of the Lutherans. Let us not doubt the outcome of this battle. God will never be defeated. The only question is, What kind of people will we prove to be in this struggle?

"Now, at the end of the school year, I wish you a pleasant vacation. I don't know if I will meet with all of you next school year. But wherever you may be, go in the name of him who has never been defeated. He will protect you and care for you!"

That is how I closed the Bible class that day. Its consequences later proved to be very important. I closed my other classes more calmly, but with the same kind of challenge: to trust in God, to cling to him, and walk with him.

At pastoral conferences I inquired how things were elsewhere and learned that they had not experienced the same difficulties. Their school years closed with a church service. From this I concluded that in a small district like Turčianské Teplice, without tradition or broad-minded officials, the officers of the ONV were driven by career ambitions. And evidently their instructions were quite clear, for at the beginning of the 1950–51 school year, no divine services were held, nor did any school year thereafter begin or conclude with worship services.

7

The Church Joins
in Its Own Suppression

Meanwhile, at the monthly pastoral conferences in Martin and at regular district conferences, the regional trustees pushed their way more and more into the forefront, attempting to replace the general pastoral conference with ÚSEK, a government-approved and -controlled association of Lutheran pastors and church administrators.

[ÚSEK, a coalition of Slovak Lutheran pastors in Czechoslovakia, was organized in 1950 by a group of pastors whose goal was to expand, on a theological basis, the loyalty of the clergy to the People's Democracy and to expand the building of socialism in the republic. (*Encyklopédia slovenská,* vol. 6, p. 216)]

In the Turiec region the chief officer of ÚSEK was Pastor Viktor Schimko, from the district of Slovenské Pravno. The members of ÚSEK were the wedge that was intended to split—as it eventually did—the previously united stand of the church and its pastors. I exposed them and polemicized against them strongly. When Schimko was in the process of preparing ground for the new law guaranteeing the economic security of the church by the state, he argued, "Do not withdraw from cooperating with the political party in power. Such cooperation will result only in advantages, while opposing it will bring you only disadvantages. You will be better off than before!"

The number of pastors in each conference who advocated cooperation with the government regulation in 1949 increased even more in 1950. They submitted detailed reports on every pastoral consultation, conference, and even private conversations. They became plain informers—sleuths—whose purpose it was to report any deviation from the statute.

At a district pastoral conference held in Ivančina, only pastors and a few pastors' wives were present. I gave a presentation on "The

Differentiation and Application of the Preaching of God's Word." In the paper I analyzed the situation in which one preaches, the hearers to whom one preaches, and the spiritual character of the preacher. I concluded that the preacher bears a great responsibility for the proclamation of God's Word, and that the effect of such preaching has a moral value. I asked, "What reward does the preacher get for this difficult and serious task?" My answer: Only a greater work load and even more difficult responsibilities!

The very next morning I was informed by an employee at the ONV in Turčianské Teplice of what I had said at the "closed" conference. Who but one of those present could have reported my remarks?

The government-approved coalition (ÚSEK) sought to enlist pastors with crude enticements, honorary dinners, recognitions, and outright monetary bribes. Bishop Čobrda complained to me at the time that a certain politician (whose name he did not divulge) justified his recruitment tactics with the sarcastic and offensive remark: "I'd like to see the pastor I could not buy for 10,000 crowns."

ÚSEK set up consultations with pastors at popular resorts, where they arranged lavish accommodations and banquets for the pastors and led them into the yoke of the organization. Such were the sadly-recalled conferences in Bojnice in the High Tatra mountains, in Luhačovice (July 2–6, 1950), and in Sliač (September 13–15, and December 4, 1950).

The invitations to these "conferences" went out first to pastors who were already "broken and tamed," then to those on the fence, and to one or two who were recalcitrant, with the intention of drawing them by subtle pressure into compliance and cooperation.

I was invited to the December 4, 1950, meeting in Sliač. I returned the invitation, noting on the margin that I could not participate because of pastoral duties. I know Andrej Žiak was present at the conference, for I ran into him on the train from Turčianské Teplice to Martin, as he was returning from the meeting. He chided me strongly for not attending the conference. He could not understand how I could possibly brush it aside. Did I not realize what the consequences might be? I said I didn't know, nor did they interest me in the least.

"Well," he said, "that's too bad," for Konvít had made a speech there that filled him with pride in the Lutheran clergy. I concluded my conversation with Žiak with the statement that I did not consider such subscribing of pastors as good for the church.

The situation between the church, its teachings and its schools, and state ideology grew ever more tense. This was evident not only to those who stuck their head in the sand, but even to those who did not care to think about it. And the church administration was helpless to do anything about it. When I drew attention to the worsening situation at pastoral conferences, many took the matter lightly and said I was dramatizing matters which in their view were otherwise normal. I could not comprehend how the situation which I considered spiritually and ecclesiastically irresponsible could be brushed off so lightly.

Viktor Schimko tried to worm my attitude out of me with what seemed an outlandish argument. "Pavel, the ŠTB are concerned about you. They visited me to check up on you, but I intervened on your behalf and convinced them to leave you alone, that you're a good boy. So you can thank me that they didn't arrest you."

He didn't expect my reaction to his statement. "So, Viktor, you have the power to decide which of us the ŠTB will investigate or leave alone! How did you manage that? Just remember this: when they lock up any of us, you will be responsible."

Pressure came from Viktor Schimko and other collaborating pastors to abolish the Association of Evangelical Pastors (SPEVAK) and replace it with ÚSEK, thereby placing it under state control. It was not a simple matter of renaming the existing organization, but of replacing it with a new spirit, that of serving an atheistic government. The state was simply resorting to its age-old method, "divide and conquer." And sadly, those who were willing to side with the state against the church were many.

Schimko also probably took part in the conferences in Luhačovice (July 3–6, 1950), in Sliač (September 13–14, 1950), and in Zvolen (November 3, 1950), where, under the protectorate of political activists, career-minded Lutherans gathered to offer their services to the state and to draw the rest of the Lutheran clergy and their congregations into their net.

The Zvolen conference was greeted by Ivan Kolesár in the name of the Constituting Committee of ÚSEK, created September 27–28, 1949. He referred to the nation-wide consultation of religious leaders that year in Žilina (where I believe Prof. Hromádka and Dean

Šenšel were present), at which some Lutheran pastors expressed the desire that, after the dissolution of SPEVAK, another organization of pastors should be formed: "We had to undo what happened last year in Piešťany." (See *CL*, 1950, pp. 364–365.)

Today we know that ÚSEK did not satisfy the desires of the Lutheran pastors in Slovakia. As proof I introduce the invitation of the church superintendent's office in Lučenec, sent June 5, 1952 (#312/52) to all pastors' offices in the Novohradský Circuit, which says, "The General Bishop's office in Communication #230/52, dated May 17, 1952, turns to the circuit officers to initiate a circuit conference of ÚSEK according to ÚSEK statute, art. 17. According to par. 13 of this statute, I am calling our spring conference of the division of ÚSEK for June 13, 1952, at 8 a.m. in the church meeting room in Lučenec. Participating in this conference will be representatives of ÚSEK, Brothers Ján Štrba and Mulutin Bágel."

So, even as late as 1952, circuit officers were called to begin the conference program of ÚSEK. It evidently took a long time for the Lutheran pastors to give in. But eventually they did submit. Pity!

I wasn't the only one who came out against ÚSEK. The majority of the pastors in our circuit agreed with me. Together with Brothers O. Vizner and D. Albini, we drew up a resolution of the Turiec circuit pastors opposing ÚSEK and wanted to send it to the Bishop General's office.

Dean Hollý said to me, "Don't sent it in your name. I'll send it as Dean with the authority of the Turiec circuit. That way it will carry more weight."

I let him persuade me to give him the resolution signed by the participants at the conference. Then I began singing Mária Royová's hymn "To Be Allowed to Live for Christ, and for Him to Die." The conference joined in, and so the meeting ended. But Viktor Schimko muttered agitatedly, "Just wait. You will yet be singing 'To Be Allowed to Live for Christ, and for Him to Die.' "

I took the remark as the thoughtless reaction of someone whose campaign for ÚSEK had failed. Well, it proved to be much more.

So what happened to the resolution? Dean Hollý did indeed send it in—together with his own application for membership in ÚSEK! By the beginning of 1950, all the Turiec circuit pastors had submitted their applications—with the exception of myself and brothers Vizner and Albini.

8

"Something" Was Drawing Nearer

I found myself deserted. Non-church groups also began closing in on me. I simply kept on working, preaching, lecturing, and evangelizing ever more earnestly, encouraged and supported by fellow-workers, students, officers, and male and female teachers. When I made note of the fact to one of my brother pastors that things were tightening around me, he said, "Didn't we warn you that it was futile to resist? *Et qui protest?*" Determined to continue doing my pastoral work, I felt something was drawing nearer.

The first indication of that "something" appeared at the very beginning of January. I failed to receive my monthly salary from the state. No one was able to tell me why. Since this was not a deciding factor for me, I didn't pursue the matter, nor did I tell my parishioners about it. Even without state support, I did not suffer want.

I sensed the "something" again when I went to the post office in Turčianské Teplice to pick up some cartons. I don't remember if it was before or after Christmas 1950. It was about four o'clock in the afternoon. I was carrying four heavy boxes out of the post office when a total stranger came up to me and offered to help me take them home for me in his car.

I found it curious that he knew I was the pastor from Háj and that the cartons were to be taken to the parsonage there. He asked me what was in the boxes, and I told him they were church annuals. I accepted the offer without question, for I would have worked up quite a sweat by the time I would have carried them a kilometer to the parsonage.

We did not converse in the car, and I thanked him when he dropped me off in front of the parsonage. Later I learned the man was ŠTB agent Pavel Gregorovič.

I had other reasons to feel that someone was following me

secretly. When I returned home after late evening Bible classes, it often seemed to me that someone was hiding behind the fence of the neighboring Roman Catholic rectory garden, taking note when and with whom I was coming home and whether anyone was staying with me. In fact, my own church members came to my office several times before church services with the frightening announcement, "Pastor, they're coming to watch what you're preaching."

I calmed their fears by saying, "Let them come. They can profit to hear a message from God's Word, and to sing and pray, or at least to witness prayers, hymns, and sermons."

It was interesting that these "hearers" later said at a National Party Committee meeting, "That pastor of yours certainly preaches well."

On February 11, 1950, I preached on the Cleansing of the Temple (Luke 19:45–46). I made the following application of the text.

"Today too the temple of God is being turned into a den of thieves. There are those who go to the house of God for reasons other than to serve God with songs, prayers, and reverent listening to God's Word. For example, those who go simply to see or be seen in Sunday clothes, or who look for something to gossip about, or who hope to find something in a sermon to report."

I mention this because in a few short days this sermon was quoted among charges brought against me before the court. It happened that at the door of the church after the sermon, I met with my former students from the *Gymnázium* in Turčianské Teplice, who were attending a different school that year and had stopped by for a visit. I welcomed them, recalled the times we had spent working together, and parted pleasantly and peacefully.

Among the students was a certain Ján Hudak, who used to come frequently to the parsonage with others to prepare for Sunday school. On one such visit, back in the Spring of 1950, as he was looking over my library, he asked me if I would lend him J. Szeberíni's *From Marx to Lenin,* and Dr. Teriansky's *Nationalism,* written by Slovak pastors from Hungary, since he too was a repatriate from Hungary. I loaned him the two books among others, but with the express caution that he should not pass them on to anyone else, as that might result in some unpleasantness. He promised, and kept his promise. But upon returning the books, he paused to say that there were certain questions concerning the books—questions which showed up later at my court hearing.

The sermon that day must also have been heard by an ŠTB agent, for statements from it were also placed in the allegations against me.

In this connection I recall a visit in Háj by a fellow pastor who was told by a seminary lecturer, "Wait and see, they'll lock up this Uhorskai." So I was the subject of conversation not only in Bratislava government and political circles, but also among church personnel. And I have the impression that someone among the church workers was identifying pastors who might be candidates for imprisonment and who should be removed for impeding the prescribed program of the church.

To confirm this suspicion of mine I recall a remark an ŠTB agent made in the presence of Dr. Lanštiak, when Brother Jozef Juráš [see Appendix C] was being fiercely hounded in Batovce: "Who is the cleverest pastor here after Juráš?" The question was aimed at determining who should be followed and removed. Lanštiak did not answer the question but said he did not know. He felt the remark was directed at him as well.

So a list of "troublesome" pastors was being prepared, with our altar brothers assisting in the project. This was borne out by subsequent events, when pastors were arrested and jailed according to a strict process of selection.

Events continued to unfold. On February 23, 1951, I was handed an injunction from the ONV in Turčianské Teplice, which forbade my admittance into any school, effective immediately. The order was signed by Ján Marčičiak, the president of the ONV. As soon as I received it, I went looking for him. He was in the midst of enrolling beginners. After several hours he took a break, and we met in his office.

He denied having issued any such prohibition. When I handed him the document with his signature on it, he shrugged his shoulders and said, "So you can't teach in the schools."

That was supposed to end the matter. But I demanded an agreement from him permitting me to find a replacement for the religion classes. This I did, with the main burden of teaching at the preparatory school and at the public school in Turčianské Teplice being assumed by my predecessor in Háj, Pastor Pavel Šolc, who was living in retirement in the town. I was also able to secure religious instruction at the remaining schools as well.

It was clear that all the assaults were now being directed at me. I went to the chairman of the ONV to ask why this method was being used against me. The chairman quibbled, not answering me directly. While I was sitting there, who appeared but ŠTB agent Pavel Gregorovič! He sat down and said nothing. I could see his presence was unnerving to Chairman Marčičiak, and the conversation was restrained.

It was then that Andrej Žiak, the delegate from the National Assembly, entered the room. When I repeated my complaint to him—that I felt restricted in my constitutional freedom—he began explaining what great merit our People's Democracy deserved for raising the social level of our people. He spoke of "the statute assuring the economic security of the church by the state, of the great concern of the government for the working class, for the progress of the JRD, industrialization and general social progress, and the duty of the church to acknowledge these realities with thanks."

I restrained myself from debating with him. I had the impression that the presence of ŠTB Gregorovič was no accident, but that he was stuck to my heels, and that I could not take one step without his knowledge. The result of my visit to the ONV was practically nil.

In my parish I was preparing for the annual congregational meeting, proceeding with the mission program as I had in the past. The meeting took place March 11, 1951.

Every annual report of mine was set in the context of the religious situation in the world, in the nation, in the Slovak Church, and in the circuit, and concerned itself with the detailed life of the congregation. I completed all the documents connected with the meeting, and on Wednesday, March 14, 1951, I sent all the correspondence to the church headquarters to meet the deadline.

9

The Trap Is Sprung

I had just finished my lunch on March 14, 1951, and had begun my preparations for the Bible hour and the Junior Evangelical Youth (DEM) meeting I was to conduct in the late afternoon and evening. Suddenly, at 1:30 P.M., five plainclothesmen in leather coats appeared beneath my windows. They entered my office and announced that they had come to search the house. They didn't present any search warrant. Nor did I ask for one. It wouldn't have changed matters even if I had.

Their first question was, "Do you have any weapons?" I never had any. Then they searched the entire house. I did not prevent them from going through the building from top to bottom, except to request that I wanted to be present with them at all times so they would not attempt to plant any incriminating evidence. They agreed.

Then they proceeded to ransack the house, all the writings, correspondence, even the waste basket. At the time I had some 1,000 books. Why, they asked, did I have so many books, why the Marxist literature: Lenin's and Marx's writings? I replied that every educated person must read books to keep up with the times, to be able to form opinions, to establish, and, if necessary, to defend one's views.

Pavel Gregorovič, who was one of the agents, commented angrily, "I suppose it's because you want to distort Marxist-Leninism and use it to fight against us."

I didn't respond. I had enough to do just keeping an eye on the five sleuths.

They kept asking me if I had any weapons. Finally I showed them a Bible and said "Yes, I have this one." That ended their questions about weapons.

After about three hours, the search ended. The place was a real mess. They had taken all my sermons, lectures, and theological works, books they considered useful, all the money in the parsonage, my personal funds and those of the congregation, and told me that I must go with them.

When I asked them where they were taking me, they said, "To the ONV." So I put on my overcoat, since it was still snowy and very cold. I asked them to leave the keys to the parsonage with the custodian, because I had no one staying with me. They refused my request, saying they knew who should get the keys, and they ordered me to get going.

So we went—with two trunk loads of sermons, lectures, books, and correspondence. The automobile was not parked in front of the parsonage but behind the church so as not to arouse the attention of the parishioners, whose opposition they feared. That was why they would not turn over the keys to the custodian.

We got into the car, a six-passenger Škoda Super. The ŠTB driver and one of the men sat in the front seat, one of them sat with me in the middle seat, and the other two occupied the back seat. All the agents were armed.

It was interesting that they expected me to resist the arrest. But I gave no resistance whatever. I was convinced of my innocence, convinced that I could defend myself against any regime, before any judge.

When we arrived in front of the ONV headquarters in Turčianské Teplice, they did not let me get out of the car. By this time my parishioners had noticed something unusual was going on. They gathered outside the car while one of the ŠTBs took the keys into the ONV office. I merely waved my hand to my church members to indicate that nothing could be done, and they dispersed. I learned later that someone sent a telegram to my parents at that time to inform them of what had happened to me.

I was then driven to Žilina, the county seat, and dropped off at the Salesian cloister, which had been transformed into the regional command post of the ŠTB. When they delivered me to the desk, I had a hard time getting oriented in the building. I only know that they led me through the main building, then through a courtyard far to the rear, where a smaller building stood. There they stuck me into a small basement room prepared for solitary confinement—about the third door along the passageway.

From that time on I lost track of the calendar and of civilian life in general. My only contact with civilization was the incarceration, the interrogation by the secret police, and the rough treatment of the government's power.

The cell was very small, only as wide as my outstretched arms, and less than three meters long, with just enough space to open the door without touching the wooden bunk.

All my belongings were left in the waiting room on the ground floor. When one of the supervisors told the agents it wasn't done that way, that every item had to be registered and signed by me, that the possessions included money and documents—they merely waved their hands that all that was unnecessary, that it was essential only that they had brought me to a place I could not leave.

Shortly thereafter they brought me my supper—tripe soup. I had no appetite, and refused it. I asked to be taken at once to the commanding officer, that I was innocent and should be released. They laughed, saying they knew how "innocent" I was, and that I would eventually get a hearing.

There was no toilet in the room. I could relieve myself only in the company of a security guard. All night long I was so restless I could not sleep. The light was turned on and off at will outside the door. I was watched through a small window in the door. On the plank bed frame there was one gray quilt to sleep on and to use as a covering. Against the bare wall, just under the ceiling, there was a small window about 30×50 cm. Around 3 A.M. there was a fearful banging in the radiator as the steam collided with the water. It was an arrogant arrangement contrived deliberately for the discomfort of the prisoners.

Around eight in the morning, they took my watch and the contents of my pockets, so I could only approximate the time of day. Then I was led again to the receiving room, where they counted the money they had taken when they picked me up. I informed them that the funds were both mine and the church's, and signed a document accordingly. The confiscated books and papers were entered into the report en masse instead of piece by piece.

I was then taken back to the cell and left to wait. No one cared to say a word to me. The only attention I got was when I was watched through the window in the door like an animal in a cage.

Something like a week passed that way. The experience was quite stressful, but I said to myself: "I'm still right. I'm not guilty of any crime. It is worth suffering something for the truth." I was able to maintain my spiritual health with regular prayers and quietly singing hymns.

My physical well-being proved more difficult to maintain. I had nowhere to wash. No toothbrush. No towel. The meager meals kept me just above the hunger level. All the while I persisted in demanding a hearing. The treatment was generally rough and arrogant, contemptuous and cynical.

About three days later I was transferred to a solitary cell at the end of the corridor. There I had a bitter experience. When the meals were being distributed, I heard a familiar woman's voice. When I glanced through the half-open door, whom did I see but one of my former students in the Teachers Academy (UA) in Martin—Jarmila Bágelová—in an ŠTB uniform! My surprise changed to cold comprehension of the fact that I remembered her as a member of a brigade in Turany, where she was suspected of being on special assignment as an informer. In fact, neither in religion classes nor in the meetings of the Association of Evangelical Youth which Jarmila attended regularly with her Catholic friend, Rosenbergová, did I ever imagine she could be an informer, especially since her grandmother who lived in Martin gave the impression of being a staunch Lutheran and a faithful church-goer. But facts are facts.

Finally, after another week had passed, I was led to a hearing. This one was remarkable! I was asked no questions. The interrogators simply recited meaningless allegations of Clero-Fascism, collaboration with the Nazis, atrocities of the Guardists [militia in the Slovak State], the SS, and other accusations similar to those directed at the leaders and policies of the Slovak State from 1939–1945. The ranting went on for hours. When I became completely tired of this, I said to myself that I had no connection with any of the groups, and that I too was persecuted by the Fascists at one time. They harangued me, silenced me, and went on prattling. I listened with an ironic smile.

Several hours later another interrogator arrived. He renewed the tirade against the People's Party, the Hlinka Guards, Fascists, Nazi collaboration, Tiso, Tuka, and Mach [the president and leaders of the former Slovak State]. I listened again with a smile, and once again rejected any ties with illegal activities. I reminded them that I was a Lutheran pastor, and that the Clero-Fascists had persecuted us Lutherans.

Eventually the interrogators took turns questioning me. When I had the same reply for all of them, they finally asked me, "Why then are you here?"

I said, "That's what I'd like to know, too!"

And so another week passed. I was left undisturbed in my cell. The "hearings" nevertheless achieved some results: I got a toothbrush, a towel, and a wash basin.

Following this reprieve from interrogation, I was transferred from solitary confinement to a larger room with several prisoners. One was a former manager of a biotechnic firm in Žilina, sentenced for some kind of fraud. Another was a swindler whose daughter was employed by the same firm, but who seemed to have been planted in the cell as an informer. Also a carpenter, who borrowed 50 crowns from my account, and a butcher accused of black-marketing, to whom I loaned 300 crowns to help pay for cigarettes he and the carpenter could not afford.

Just before Easter they brought in some farmers from a region inundated by a dam, and another spy who claimed to be a Ukrainian.

In the larger ward, we passed much of the time talking. To the farmers I expounded on the Easter texts in a kind of homily, and I sang Easter hymns which they appreciated. For the others I sang patriotic songs. All this the guards observed with interest.

One of the guards later brought a chessboard and asked me to play a few games with him, which I did. I soon discovered that he was spying on me, probing my mind, challenging my intellect, and measuring my views, my character, and my convictions.

Another security guard brought me a Bible and a tract entitled "Words of Comfort"—secretly, since he said it came from the cousin of a certain Mazáková from the Lutheran parsonage in Žilina. Like a true sister, she sent me a change of underwear, which I needed badly, having spent three weeks in custody with only the clothes I was wearing when arrested. (In general, the hygiene in the place was deplorable.) To this day I do not know if this was a favor of the secret agent or of that "sister." Of one thing there could be no doubt—the agent delivered the underwear and picked up the soiled linens to have them washed. Then he would return my own laundered linens and pick up the borrowed ones. One day he whispered to me that this favor had been reported to the director, and that it could cause trouble. The laundering stopped, but I was allowed to keep the Bible. It went with me into my imprisonment.

The same agent informed me that my parishioners had gone to the headquarters of the ŠTB in Žilina to intercede for me. Quite a number of them—20 or more—went to the director, who chewed them out for getting involved in my case, telling them that if they didn't have enough to do, there was plenty of work to occupy them in the Union of Agricultural Workers (JRD). He even threatened to lock them up, too. Yet they persisted in pleading for my release, insisting I had committed no criminal offense. Eventually they had to leave without success.

I must note here that prior to my arrest I had discussed with my parishioners the possibility of my arrest. The elderly custodian, Michal Sunka, viewed the brewing situation very naively. "We won't surrender you," he pledged. "We'll resist them. We'll guard you in the parsonage, or we'll hide you in some home or in the mountains."

I tried to persuade him with a smile that his attitude was unrealistic; that neither he, nor the community, nor the church had the power to stand up against the might of the State. I said they would only harm themselves unnecessarily. They would also risk being arrested, and they endangered me by implying that I was urging them to insurrection. In the event of my arrest, I advised them to intervene reasonably through official channels. As it happened, no intervention helped, though they did build up my moral fortitude.

10

What Were My Crimes?

Everything that was happening convinced me that the investigators had nothing concrete against me, because they resorted to lumping me together with Fascists, Nazi collaborators, and Populists. They had to identify a specific fault, and someone would have to instruct them as to what crime this Lutheran pastor/catechete/professor actually committed.

This then became the focus of the ŠTB efforts. They followed procedures intended to get something out of me in a hearing that could be entered into the records as grounds for imprisonment. Something like:

- I led secret anti-Marxist groups;
- in my Bible classes I was refuting dialectical materialism in an anti-Marxist manner;
- I was distributing anti-Marxist literature to my students;
- I had Marxist literature in my library, which I was studying in order to undermine Communism more successfully;
- I was enticing students to the parsonage and at various retreats and conferences to train them for anti-government activities; and
- I was acting against the Socialist Youth League (SSM) and slandering them.
- In general, that I was a sworn enemy of the People's Democratic system, that I was claiming in my Bible classes that religion was persecuted in our country, that I called workers "dogs," and that in a certain sermon I had labeled functionaries and members of the SSM as thieves.

That is what was pounded into me day and night.

The preparation for this stacked-deck hearing began with the entry into the interrogation room by Vlado Danek, who issued strict orders that from that moment on I must not sit or lie down or sleep—only stand! So I stood for two days and two nights without food, to the point of total exhaustion. My feet swelled up; I became weak. In short, I was completely drained.

Then the examination began.

It was really more than an examination; it was a subtle pressure to make me admit to all of the charges. I must confess that the endless allegations summoned up in me a great revival of spirit and energy. Though drained physically, I reacted vigorously to every charge. I was able to recall in detail every lecture, sermon, and class—and quoted them accurately in contrast to their distortions. I introduced data as to when and where I said or did anything. Thus they scrutinized my sermons, lectures, senior and junior youth meetings, preparations for youth conferences, conversations with the ONV, and what not—to the limits of tedium.

I explained and rejected their allegations as follows:

● Leading anti-Marxist groups

I led no such groups. I did do mission work in various youth organizations according to the requirements of my pastoral call, in which these duties were spelled out. I was thereby training young people in the spirit of the Gospel. Since that is the primary obligation of the church, it could not have been a criminal offense. The church is not outlawed in our country. The church is Biblical, and the Bible is not banned. If this were the case, one would have to condemn all pastors, catechetes, church members, and all believers, for they are all as "guilty" as I am. I was teaching Marxist theories only insofar as the Bible teaches them, and I was anti-Marxist only insofar as the Bible is anti-Marxist.

● Disputing dialectical materialism in religion classes

In my instruction I followed approved programs. In dogmatics I lectured on the fundamental doctrines of the Christian faith, and instilled in students Christian views, which I compared with non-Christian and anti-Christian concepts. My motto was the Biblical precept: "Examine everything; cling to the best." In addition I emphasized why I hold Christian convictions and why I reject other views. I was teaching and training my students to think, but I forced no views on anyone.

● Distributing anti-Marxist literature

I never gave my students any kind of anti-Marxist literature. I did loan some books to J. Hudak on the condition that he would not lend them to anyone else. In time he returned the books to me, not having loaned them to anyone. As a matter of fact, the books he borrowed have never appeared on any index. The two authors are here in Slovakia. Not only has no one condemned the books for anything, but our own publishing houses issued the books with the approval of the censors. What kind of transgression had I then committed by possessing the books and permitting someone to read them?

● Marxist literature in my library

In my library I had some Marxist literature that I studied. Is the study of Marxism criminal? Is it not in fact advocated? The fact that I was clarifying my position on the basis of it and over and against it is self-evident. No educated person at the present time can possibly help but know what Marxists are saying; and why should I, a teacher and trainer of the future intelligentsia, not be familiar with it?

● Visits of students in my office and my participation in organized outings

I am unaware of *luring* pupils into my office. That is a lie! On the other hand, I did welcome their visits, as any pastor should, whose parsonage is open to church members and non-members alike. Those who visited my office certainly left with nothing harmful. All pedagogical systems in the world recommend such contacts between teacher and pupil.

As for organizing trips and retreats, I did so in conformity to school policy. They served to broaden students' knowledge and helped in the formation of character. There was no hint of anti-government indoctrination. I too love my country. I fought for this country. It is a country of all believing Christian citizens.

● Attitude toward the Socialist Youth League (SSM)

I was not a worker for the SSM. As a pastor and catechete, I had other obligations toward my pupils than to direct them to the SSM. My calling was to train them in Christian faith and life. Though I did not hinder them from participating in SSM activity, I did, however, reproach them for misusing SSM activities and privileges, as a number of them did, by staying out late at night and, in some cases, engaging in drunkenness and orgies.

My sermon in Háj on February 11, 1951, regarding the cleansing of the temple in Jerusalem by our Lord, was in no way aimed at the SSM activists who happened to be in church that day without my knowledge. The expression "den of thieves" appears in the text.

(See the earlier report of this incident.) Such a misunderstanding of the expression is a distortion of the sense and purpose of the sermon.

● Claiming religion is persecuted in our country

I never spoke specifically about the persecution of the church in our land. The source of this allegation was my explanation to my students in Turčianské Teplice as to why we were forbidden by the ONV to conduct a closing worship service at the end of the 1950–51 school year. I showed them the decree. Strange, is it not, that our government guarantees religious freedom, yet when we want to go to church, we are forbidden to do so? This was not the first time such a ban appears in church annals.

● I called workers "dogs"

This is an evil-minded falsehood. I was quoting an old saying from Klein-Tesnoskalský's biography of Matthew Bahýl'—"The moon is not hurt when dogs bark at it"—in the sense that fighting God is futile. In that connection and in that sense I quoted Psalm 2:1–4 on that particular occasion.

The investigators were very interested in ensnaring as many people as possible into my case. They questioned them as to who were my friends, with whom I associated, who assisted me in my work. I perceived their intentions and denied having any connections with anyone. "I associated with members of my church," I said, but did not mention any names. "I visited my parishioners, as my pastoral office demands."

They knew I had meetings of the junior youth at the home of L. Rác. They also verified that I also visited him privately, and they questioned me as to whether he was a Yugoslav. He himself is not, though he did have a Yugoslavian connection. His father-in-law came from Serbia and migrated to Slovakia prior to World War I, and had died long ago, long before I met the family. The ŠTB would have liked to trap me in some connection with Yugoslavia, for at that time the Titoist deviation from the Soviet bloc was taking place, as a result of which many innocent Slovaks were condemned and interned, e.g., Mirko Petrovič, a Lutheran pastor who was sentenced to more than 20 years.

Despite the relentless efforts of the ŠTB to create some anti-government group around me, I did not implicate anyone in this sad situation. During the interrogation, I came to the understanding and conviction that it was not a matter of [establishing] guilt or an actual criminal act, but of liquidating or removing anyone who stood in the path of Marxist ideology. This is proved by the following experience.

I was interrogated severely—by the use of physical force and psychological pressure—with the intention of breaking my character and weakening most of my moral strength. They shouted at me, called me names, forced me to do strenuous exercises, and "hung me on the wall." They threatened me with guns and clubs. I was so worn out I could not lie or sit or stand. Ultimately I fell to the floor, unable to move my limbs or my tongue, not even to utter a sound, much less to speak. But—and for this especially I thank God—I did not lose consciousness for a moment, never shed a tear, never groaned.

Following two days and two nights of standing, the interrogation continued piecemeal for I don't remember how long; I had lost all track of time. The questioners took turns after several hours. When one got tired, a second one came. When the second became tired, a third; and after the third, a fourth. And then they went around again. I defended myself, saying I was completely exhausted. Then the interrogator said cunningly—as if he were following a guide-book—"Well then, let's take a break. Let's do some exercises." And he barked, "Squat! Stand!"

I played along with the strategy. I squatted. I stood up. When I slowed down, he brandished a stick. So I did at least 20 more squats before I collapsed on the floor. He shouted at me, raving at his helpless victim. I could only listen and keep quiet and try to catch my breath.

When I roused myself from the floor, the examination contin-ued. I protected myself against their methods by saying to them, "You are wrong. You have no right to treat me like this."

"Do you mean I'm mistaken and that I don't have the right?" he shouted. "The person who has the power has both the power and the right. To the wall!"

Actually he stood me several feet from the wall and placed my outstretched arms against it. I was forced to stand like that until my waist gave way and I fell to the floor. Again more shouts, curses, threats, and even harsher violence.

Then for a while I was left alone. It was quiet. But soon the silence was shattered by sounds from the floor above: cries, moans, sobs, beatings, and pleadings. I don't know how long this lasted. Then the interrogator would say, "See, this is how I can deal with you, and I will! So talk! I'll teach you what you should answer. You will sing your confession like a bird. And you will say what I decide."

Thereupon the bullying resumed, repeating what they wanted to force me to say. But I refused to comply. I denied all the allegations and disputed them. The agent began to rant and tore up his notes. And again the same routine. On and on until he tired.

It was then that I personally experienced the unimaginable act of self-condemnation which prominent political leaders were willing to perform. They would eventually condemn themselves, confessing to crimes they had not committed. I reminded myself of this and kept telling myself, "I must not give in like that; I must not break down. After all, I am innocent. The truth is on my side. I've never been mixed up in politics. All I did was carry on my pastoral ministry and work conscientiously in the mission field. That kind of activity has a high moral benefit to society. One must not stain it with weakness and betrayal."

Now I remember—that agent's name was Matula.

Then ŠTB agent Rudo Marčan came into the room. He saw my totally wretched condition and began to pity me. He reminded me of my social origin, that I came from a poor farm family of eleven children, and that I was still unwilling to support the communists who were helping to eradicate poverty and wanted only to help me and others like myself. Did I not see that they had only my good at heart? Did I not understand that they had to use force to get me to enjoy those benefits, just as a kitten has to have its face pressed into a bowl of milk, and even though it is afraid and angry and sputters, eventually it will start to drink. Similarly I should give up my unreasonable resistance. I should join the Marxists, and everything would be in order.

He went on to say that I really had no fault, that I was very intelligent, gifted, and educated, and that I could well continue with my education. The new system would open up possibilities for me that the church could never provide. Anyone could see what abilities I had, what moral character and strength—and so on, praising me to the skies.

I just listened in silence. When he asked me for my reaction, I said, "I am not the first, nor the last, to be faced with such a decision. Let me give you an example from the political life of the Czech poet and political leader, K. Havliček-Borovský. When the Austrian Germans investigated him, and pressured and enticed him to accept the notion of Pan-Germanism, he declared, 'Promise me everything and threaten me, but I will not be a traitor. German? I am a Czech!' With that he permitted himself to be condemned and sent into exile. Furthermore, my Lutheran bishop, Dr. Karol Kuzmány, taught me in his poem 'In Praise of the Noble':

> Whom gifts cannot corrupt, nor terror drown:
> For him my song with glory shall resound.

"I have no reason to depart from these examples of integrity. In the service of Christ I am in a good kind of service. I am not aware of any wrongdoing for which I should be judged by you!"

"Well, if you aren't willing, that's your business. I merely wanted to help you. I wanted to treat you differently than my predecessor. If you don't accept my method, I will have to deal with you by his." And again came more threats, distortions of facts, revisions of the report. In the end, I confessed no fault, and they proved no fault.

I have no idea how long, how many days and nights the merry-go-round lasted. After that wave of examinations, there came a longer respite. I had peace for several days and nights.

I was returned to a room with several other detainees, who looked at me with expressions of horror and approached me very fearfully. I was unable to answer them; I could only fall down on the plank cot and sleep. The guards came by, and I continued sleeping like a log. They didn't bother to wake me up. I don't know how long I slept, but when I awoke, I was given something to eat. And I ate.

The old farmers there came to me with tears, asking what had been done to me. All I could say was, "They investigated me."

When the supervisor came around later with something to eat, he reproached me: "Why are you so hard-headed?" I did not answer.

Before long another Sunday rolled around. It must have been after Easter. The ŠTB was nowhere to be seen or heard. Only the staff were there. At the time women from the detention ward were being recruited to assist in distributing meals. They were nuns, professors from some cloister or *Gymnázium*. Among them a Mária

Surianská, a fiftyish directress; another former abbess, Schaefferová, about 70 years old; and a thirtyish religious named Chladná, who had taught philosophy. As the youngest one, Chladná was chosen to help with the meals.

When she brought the dinner to our room, she looked about to see if the guard was nearby and asked hurriedly, "Which of you is that Lutheran pastor?"

I said, "I'm the one. Why?"

"Did you know that in my interrogation, they used you as a dissuading example, saying I have as hard a head as you. I felt flattered that they compared me with you," she said.

"Did they beat you too?" I asked.

"Yes, but I held out. Especially when they compared me to you."

We became very close at that moment.

I asked her, "Sister, do you have *The Way of the Cross* with you? I'd like to use it for my meditations."

"I don't have it with me, but I'll find it for you," she said. And indeed she brought me a copy gladly and willingly.

This was my first contact behind the backs of the ŠTB. During my internment, I became quite proficient in this conspiracy.

Furthermore, in my contemplation of *The Way of the Cross,* I came to the conviction that the Lord had chosen me for this path, too. I deemed it important to walk it obediently, faithfully, and with integrity. It doesn't matter if the goal is near or distant. I knew I would reach the goal, for not everyone who runs receives the victor's laurel, but he who runs faithfully (2 Tim. 2:5). Hence I would have to fight to the end, and uprightly.

For two or three days we had peace. Now and then someone came to check the cell, but they didn't ask me anything. Then the supervisor came to me with a proposal: Would I care to go to an upper area of the building to clean up after the bricklayers who were doing some repair work there? I said I would be glad to. I had the impression that he was feeling sorry for me and wanted to give me a little more freedom of movement.

There was nothing special to do there, just sweeping a little rubble, placing it into a container, and cleaning up with a dust cloth afterward. It could be done in 15 minutes.

I played at the job for over an hour. When I took the wastebasket out into the yard, I had to go through a corridor. A woman staff member looked out of a doorway, and when she noticed me, she gasped in surprise and stood transfixed in the doorway. I went on with my task, going out into the yard, emptied my sweepings and came right back.

Upon my return, I saw two girls there now look at me in fright and whisper something. I didn't recognized them, and I don't know if they recognized me. They may have known only that I was the Lutheran pastor under investigation. When I finished the job, I stood in the doorway and waited for the supervisor. Meanwhile the girls were watching me from their own doorway. I must have been quite a spectacle to them—detained for weeks, unshaven, not very clean, and rather ragged-looking. I did, however, retain a lively look and a quick perception.

Just then I heard the whistle of the train from Rajec. I looked at the gate to the yard. About five steps from where I stood, there was an ordinary wooden fence. I could have jumped over it easily. For a moment a temptation occurred to me: No one is guarding me; I could escape. But I dismissed the thought as ridiculous. Where would I go? And why? I had no reason to run away. Nevertheless, I was overcome with a nostalgia such as I had never felt in my cell.

It must have been two hours before my supervisor came to return me to my cell. On the way I told him what I was tempted to do while alone upstairs. He got scared and asked me if I would have run away.

I told him, "You can see I'm still here." However, he did not let me out any more after that.

In the meantime the cellmates were changed. The guard brought in a Roman Catholic priest, who told me he had been arrested because he had asked soldiers on leave what the morale was among the troops. This was considered espionage. He fussed and wept and begged, while the ŠTB agents treated him with utter contempt. He was released in a couple of days and moved from his station in Ludrová to Dolný Kubín, in what I suspect was a plea bargain he made with the government. I remember meeting him on my release from prison, when I went to visit my brother in Dolný Kubín. Evidently one could escape punishment in several ways. For me, however, in the detention camp, I preferred the enmity and hatred of the ŠTB to their contempt and "mercy."

Some days later the ŠTB examination resumed. For them it was unchanged, but on my part it was different. From the previous round I learned that it didn't matter to them how long and how much they would torture me, but to me it did. And so after being "hung on the wall," I collapsed to the floor in a short time. Similarly, when I did a couple of squats, I collapsed again. I thought to myself, I must save my strength. They raged in vain, as I did not allow myself to be broken as before. Then a kind of deadening set it.

After more than three weeks of brutal interrogation, and after an unsuccessful struggle to obtain a correct and true deposition, and after what seemed to me a useless resistance to the distortion of my statements—I signed the report, such as it was. I signed it, convinced that I would be better able to defend my position in court than here, where nothing is right, where there is only self-will and ill will. If one were to compare the "confession/report" with what I presented as my explanation of the allegations, one would be amazed at the combinations of truths and falsehoods, and the variations on the lies themselves. Well, I signed the document. Let others judge it as they will.

The interrogators were happy to have the report ready. To me it was a matter of indifference. It annoyed me, however, when they told me laughingly that I could have saved myself the lengthy examination, since it turned out their way after all.

11

On to the Next Stop

In a few more days, somewhere around the 22nd or 23rd of April, 1951, at about 11 A.M., the guard brought me some tea and dry potatoes, and told me to eat because I was going away. When I asked him where, he said he didn't know, but I should eat, because it would do me good. So I filled up on the dry potatoes and washed them down with the tea.

Then I packed my things—that is, I put on the coat and cap they brought me. From the closet, I took the Bible one of the ŠTBs had brought me. And I was ready.

I was led out into the yard, where a dark green military ambulance with a red cross on it stood. They opened the door and motioned me to get in. In the ambulance there were already six nuns, among them the ones I mentioned earlier. We were escorted by three ŠTBs and a driver.

Since the sisters knew me already, we greeted each other almost like old friends. After some small talk, the conversation turned serious. I thanked them for *The Way of the Cross* they had loaned me. I showed them the Bible and the *Words of Comfort*. Whether out of fear of the guards or for some other reason, they did not take them into their hands. Instead, they asked me to read something to them.

I read the account of Jesus' anointing in Mark 14:8, pointing to Jesus' honoring Mary's deed, saying, "She did what she could." ŠTB agent P. Mačan listened to the reading without malice. As I read the Passion texts to the sisters, Mačan requested that I read something to him, too.

I said, "Listen, this is for you, too," and by coincidence we came to the account of Judas' betrayal of our Lord. The sisters smiled, but the agent did not take it as a personal reference to him, which indeed it was not meant to be.

I still had no idea where we were going. Only when we stopped somewhere in Trenčín did I notice that we were headed for Bratislava. The sisters confirmed the fact. The ride to Bratislava passed quite peacefully. The circumstances were not conducive to extended conversation. Nevertheless, the sisters provided me with a moral stimulus. It felt good to be in their company after the distress with the ŠTBs, even though we conversed little.

We arrived in Bratislava at dusk. Our ambulance pulled up at No. 2 Ruská Street. That was the entrance to the Bratislava state prison, the legendary "krajzak" connected to the Palace of Justice. The ŠTBs arranged for our van to enter the street beyond the first gate. There the ambulance stopped, and we remained in it. Ahead of us there were still a number of latticed gates.

We waited there for nearly half an hour. Then we were taken to a walk through many barred doors. After a while we arrived in the reception room to be presented. I don't recall the details any more, what all they entered into our records, but obviously everything the ŠTBs had brought along with us. The ceremony lasted about an hour.

When the registering was completed, I was called to go with a new guard. I parted from the sisters with a sincere word of greeting, for which the guard criticized me, saying, "Who do you think you are to take such liberties as a prisoner?" I was not surprised by that or anything else any more. I had graduated from a hard school.

On the way to my prison cell, the guard stopped in a sort of vestibule, placed me face to the wall and ordered me to wait. The supervisor reminded the guard that I was not to go to my cell unless I first went through a sanitary bath.

The guard led me to a communal shower room. However, there was no warm water. So he sprayed me with cold water. The regulation was fulfilled: I had passed the cleansing bath.

Then the warden told me the number of my cell on the upper main floor. I've forgotten the number. There I was stuck into a cell, and I had my place of residence.

A detainee was already there in the cell. He was Airman Captain Ján Pecho, who had served in Poprad, where he was also arrested. He had a wife from Veľká, where she lived with her parents and their four-year-old daughter. The fact that he was from Poprad served to draw us to each other and to eliminate the ubiquitous distrust among prisoners.

After about an hour of conversation, everything was in order. Meanwhile, the prisoners in the neighboring cell pounded vainly on the wall to find out what was going on, having heard the cell door open and close. When I asked my cellmate what the banging was about, he gave me an evasive reply, saying he did not know, that it was nothing really. After our confidence was established, he tapped out a message in Morse code on the wall, that the cell had received an addition, a Lutheran pastor.

To my relief, I found my roommate to be an honorable person, and I treated him as such from the moment I entered the cell. I had pleasant memories of our stay together in prison. To this day I can say he did not disappoint me. The ŠTBs didn't bring me any supper that day, and Pecho had nothing to offer me. So we spent the time talking. From him I learned my first rules for prison survival, how I was to behave toward other prisoners and toward the secret police: that it was useless to believe them, and especially not to disclose anything to them, and how to communicate with fellow-prisoners without being noticed by the ŠTB.

I learned the Morse code from him in one afternoon. He had been in prison for some months and had contrived a way of concealing a needle and some thread he had made by unraveling a torn sock, and a stub of a pencil.

I in turn sang him sacred hymns and prayed regularly with him. Several of them became his favorites, e.g., "Christe sanctorum," and "The day you gave us, Lord, has ended." We made a good twosome: a Lutheran pastor and a Roman Catholic layman.

I tolerated the imprisonment better there than in Žilina. The conditions were peaceful. Spiritually and physically I was able to rest more, and was more relaxed than before my arrest. In those days I worked to the point of exhaustion. At the end of some Sundays I was completely drained. Now I could feel my energy rebuilding. It was a good sign.

Our daily schedule went something like this: 6 A.M., wake-up, personal hygiene, making the bed, and breakfast at approximately 7 A.M. Around ten o'clock, a 20- to 30-minute walk. Then a wait for lunch at noon. After lunch, waiting for supper at about 4 P.M., then a late evening snack at about 8 P.M. in the winter, and around 9 P.M. in the summer.

When we reached the stage of trustees, we were given work to do. We would pack seed packets for planting, make flags for May Day, cut soles for rubber sandals, and do other odd jobs. Naturally, we were not allowed to keep the scissors in our cells.

There was plenty of time for thinking and conversing. During that period I wrote several poems, e.g., "My Cell, My Four-Walled World" and [included here] "I Am Building a Temple:"

> I am building a temple.
> Out of suffering and pain
> I am building a temple.
> Out of thoughts and yearnings
> I am building a temple.
> Out of the blessings and grace of my Lord
> I am building a temple.
> Out of faithful service and meekness
> I am building a temple.
>
> Bless it, Lord,
> And dwell in it.
>
> Out of my life
> I am building a temple.
> Out of the life of your church
> I am building a temple.

With such a daily schedule, it was no wonder that I tried to make contact with neighboring cells by means of the Morse code. It was a pleasant distraction. The walls were alive with the continuous sounds of Morse code signals. When I mastered the technique, I spent hours with my ear against the table that folded down from the wall.

I would decode messages aloud to my colleague. The reports informed us as to the latest arrivals in the prison, who had a trial and how long a sentence was imposed, who was president of the Parliament, who was the prosecutor, and what each of them was like, what the papers *Pravda* and *Rudé Právo* were saying, what Radio Free Europe and London were broadcasting. We received regular reports at 5:00, 7:00, and 8:00, then after our walking exercise period, around 11 A.M.; after lunch at 1:00, and after work at 5 and 7 P.M., and after the evening snack at 9 P.M.

It was interesting to be integrated into this prison life. Obviously, sending and receiving messages was strictly forbidden and punishable, but such transgressions had to be proved. When one person was sending or receiving messages, the other had to be on the lookout for guards.

One day after our walk, Pecho was communicating with the next cell, and I was watching for the guards. When I heard the guard's footsteps in the corridor, I signalled him to stop sending. The footsteps receded, and I signaled him to resume sending. Once, however, I did not hear the guard approaching. Suddenly the window in the door flew open, and the guard shouted, "You were sending messages!" It was the head guard, Ondrej Kútny.

Pecho hid the spoon he was using for signalling in his sleeve, took a position at the door and announced in an official voice, "Two investigators in the cell; everything's in order!"

The guard insisted, "You were sending messages!"

Pecho denied just as vehemently, "No!"

And I insisted (truthfully) that *I* had not been transmitting. Unable to prove his accusation, the guard left with a threat.

When lunch came, the guard brought us lentil soup. We waited for what would come next. He took our cups, left, and in a little while we heard the door window rattle. We figured we were going to be hauled off to the correction room. But no. To our surprise, the guard handed us two more cups of soup. So we received a double lunch.

Pecho recovered quickly and pointed out the lesson we learned. Had we confessed, we would have been punished. But since we admitted nothing, we got a double lunch.

From then on, however, he was afraid to send any more messages. So the function of radio-telegrapher fell to me, and I was happy to do it. I did not do the transmitting with a spoon but with my finger, which was less noisy and faster. Dashes were indicated with a colon, tapped with two fingers. I soon developed a pretty decent system, so that I was able to match the fastest telegraphers. But the tips of my index and middle fingers developed callouses.

Before long I was able to send and receive messages so successfully that the guards never caught me, even though they stood behind the door or watched through the peep-hole. When I was transferred to another cell to room with Dr. Martin Hano, my countryman from Ozdín, a physician, urologist, and surgeon; and later to another cell with Gubánin and Kudašík—I demonstrated the valuable services of a reporter.

My meeting with Dr. Hano was indeed special. The guard had taken me to a cell somewhere on the second floor. The door was open when he took me into the room and left me there without closing the door. After a while, a man of medium height came into the room. I'll never forget his appearance: close-cropped hair, exhausted, breathless, and thin, with a sharp nose and glaring eyes. I stood before him embarrassed, greeted him, and introduced myself. He merely uttered an inarticulate sound, in which I could only make out something like "H . . . n." I again asked him his name. And again I could not understand him. The third time it sounded like "Hano." I repeated the name to him and asked if he was the Martin Hano from Ozdín. Only then did we somehow make a connection and begin drawing closer to each other.

He had already spent 24 months in the detention center. Inhumanely tortured, nerves shattered, he had to undergo a cure as a prisoner. He related unbelievable experiences of the transmission of electromagnetic waves in the vicinity of the cot where he slept, after which he suffered terrifying nightmares. He imagined the torturing of his wife, how she bled and screamed that they were weakening his will and forcing him to confess to what the interrogators wished him to admit. He was driven past exhaustion to the point of suicide.

We talked a great deal, prayed together—rather, I was praying with him—and I sang him sacred hymns. The following moved him deeply: "O, Dear Lord," and "O Come, O Come, Year of the Lord."

As he opened up to me, he faulted the church for its stagnation, the clergy for their superficiality, shallowness, and unproductive work, their lack of enthusiasm and joy, living the fixed stereotype, weak in pronouncing judgment, and lacking the Holy Spirit. Nevertheless, though he professed respect and love for the church, I am unable to characterize his religion, his spiritual life, or his faith.

We were together for such a short time, two or three weeks at the most. I found him feeling very wronged, overly sensitive, and suspecting the ŠTB of trying to poison him. And, he was always very, very hungry! When he received his portion of bread for the day in the morning—a piece about the size of a fist—he gulped it down with coffee and then had nothing left for the rest of the day. He was surprised that I divided my portion into three pieces and wondered if that would be enough for the day. Even so, we lacked sufficient food.

When you add to the hunger the harsh interrogation, the guards' coarse treatment, and the widespread injustice, no wonder that it took an extra amount of moral strength to discipline oneself to apportion the daily allotment of food to last the entire day. Dr. Hano was weak in this respect. He could not bear shortages. Both he and I lost weight. We were all weak, and those who were in prison longer were weaker than the new arrivals. And Hano had been detained 20 months longer than I!

Hano was continually in conflict with the guards, complaining about stomach cramps and diarrhea, then repeating the routine: gulping down his food, getting sick, going to the prison doctor. He simply could not bear the injustices of the system.

Shortly thereafter I became a cellmate with Gubánin, a soldier and bricklayer, and with Kudašík, a mountaineer who pastured horses and farmed, and was arrested as a member of the Bandera insurrectionists. I do not wish to relate their stories, crimes, investigations, and tortures. Poor Kudašík still had marks of an ŠTB's boots on his stomach and bruises from beatings on his ankles and the soles of his feet. He cried like a child and had a hard time dealing with his imprisonment.

It was evident in his case that a simple person accustomed to living outdoors finds it much harder to endure internment than an intellectual. Kudašík was helped considerably by my comfort and was soothed by prayers, the singing of hymns, and devotional meditations.

He also enjoyed my reception and transmission of messages from and to walls to the right and left, above and below our cell. In the cell to our left, there were a Roman Catholic priest, Sámeľ, and a Catholic chaplain, Lenko, from Liptov. From them I received by Morse code the pericopal Gospel and Epistle lessons for the entire church year. These came from a smuggled breviary they had found in a straw mattress.

I confess that I have indulged myself in reciting these experiences in order to present a picture of how other prisoners did nor did not endure their sentences. It is time to return to my own case and concerns.

Shortly after I arrived at the detention center, I was summoned to sign my registration documents. At the time I had no idea how I would be hurt when they classified as "incriminatory possessions" such things as all the money I had when I was arrested (some 53,000 crowns), books, sermons, lectures, various writings, and other odds and ends. I was not allowed to withdraw any funds from my account, not even an allowance for everyday needs.

It took at least three weeks of detention before I was given a small tablet and a pencil with a note that I could write home 26 words of harmless content. If I wrote anything harmful, the censor would erase it. However, they did not define what was considered harmful. That was my first communication with my family—three months after my detention.

About a month later, I was called into a room where a guard, the ex officio defense attorney, Dr. Vladimir Šrobár, and I were alone. The defender inquired about my criminal offense. I said I knew of none. At that he produced my "deposition." He asked me whether I could summon some people who would clarify my case and help me. I offered no names whatever, because I did not want to cause anyone any unpleasantness by dragging them into my case, and also because I thought doing so would be worse for me as well.

For a long time thereafter, no one paid attention to me. Sometime that summer, the president of the panel of the state court in Bratislava, Jozef Pavelka, had me summoned to a hearing. He read me my charges and had me sign an affidavit that I had been shown the document and was familiar with it. However, they did not leave me with a copy of the charges, nor did they allow me to make any comments. In fact, I could not make notes either, since I had no paper, pencil, or pen.

That was all there was to the meeting—simply that I was informed of the charges prior to a court hearing. As I remember, what Pavelka read to me did not correspond to what the prosecutor, Dr. P. Winter, read to me in court. Pavelka would not tell me when the hearing would take place. He merely informed me that I would have an unofficial defender, whom I already knew.

And so I waited for the hearing convinced that I was innocent and would therefore be exonerated. Actually, I took the opportunity to review the charges. Since I had nothing to make notes with, I thanked God for a good memory and prepared my responses in my head.

Only now do I see how pitifully little I knew about court procedures. I had no idea what rights a defendant has, and so I could not know if the trial was conducted correctly or incorrectly. I was reconciled to the fact that I stood completely helpless before a governmental power. I had no power to protest its actions or decisions. I kept believing I would find a common denominator in questions of good and evil. But I had fooled myself.

Toward the end of July, they played an unpleasant game with me. In order to put an end to my boredom, they submitted a somewhat vague summons to appear at a court hearing July 31, 1951, regarding an anti-government matter. I waited. The deadline arrived. But there was no court hearing; it turned out to be some kind of smoke-screen.

Still, the experience taught me a definite lesson: I learned for the first time that I would be tried for an anti-government activity. I laughed inwardly, because I was unaware of any such offense.

By this time I was physically drained. This must have affected my eyesight particularly. When we went out into the courtyard for our daily walk, striding briskly in a circle separated from one another by eight or ten paces, driven by the guards like horses in a corral, I became fatigued in ten minutes. When we walked for twenty minutes, I could hardly make it back to my cell. On the walks I noticed that I could see the man in front of me indistinctly. I could not make out the lines in his face, but only the general outline. I asked for a physical examination.

Wearing my glasses to the doctor's office, I could recognize some cellmates along the way, such as Novotný from Bardejov. But when I told the doctor I thought I was losing my sight and asked for some vitamins, he said he had no medicines for my problem, that it was the result of exhaustion and would improve once I was free and living in better conditions. I could only sigh, "When will I ever be free, since I haven't yet been tried?" He merely shrugged and dismissed me. That is an example of the care we received in prison.

12

What Was Happening on My Behalf Outside?

What was being done about my case by my congregation and my family? My family understood better than I that I was trapped in a political process. They knew of no criminal offenses, and so they appealed to the church leadership, to the still-to-be-ordained general bishop, J. Chabada (1915–1970). They asked him what crimes I had committed. He reassured them that I was guilty of nothing and that, on the occasion of his ordination as bishop in Zvolen, I would be present in my gown as a full-fledged pastor.

The ordination of Bishop General J. Chabada and that of General Superintendent Andrej Žiak took place October 11, 1951. The bishop was not being honest. When the representatives of the Háj parish (probably Ján Chorváth, a trustee from Dolná Štubňa, Ján Kleskeň, a trustee from Vieska, Jozef Sýkora, a trustee from Čremošné, and others) went to consult with him, he told them, "What Uhorskai has cooked up, he now has. He committed some very dangerous anti-government offenses. It is impossible to help him anymore!"

The bishop refused to discuss the case with them any further. It's a wonder he did not expel them for having the nerve to come to him with such a matter.

Of course, the representatives could not imagine what kind of anti-government activity I had conducted. I had been in daily contact with them. They were witnesses of every aspect of my ministry and still knew of no anti-state actions. Helplessly they went back home and informed the parishioners of their reception by General Bishop Chabada.

When I compare what the bishop told my sister—that I had done nothing criminal and that I would take part in his installation in Zvolen as a full-fledged pastor—with what he told the delegates from the parish—that I had committed "dangerous anti-government acts" and that "it was impossible for anyone to help me"—it is evident that he contradicted himself. Actually, I think he knew nothing at all about any criminal offense.

I prefer to believe that he was intimidated by political officials who found it convenient to frighten someone who was seated in the bishop's chair by their good graces with the charge that Lutheran pastors were an anti-government element in society, and that he should never forget by whose graces he occupied his office. Actually, he could know what every "progressive" pastor knew about me, i.e., that I did not agree with the course the church was taking and that I wanted to preserve the Christian character of the church.

My parishioners remembered something else from that visit. They attended all my court hearings and never heard anything about anti-state activities. They came to the conclusion that Bishop Chabada's judgment was harsher than that of the court, because he condemned me for crimes I had never committed. With that he lost the respect of my parishioners altogether.

This instance served to show to what lengths one could be led by slavish obedience to political forces, who were less concerned about truth and justice than about power. And whatever defied that power was obviously bad.

Inwardly I was preparing for the court hearing. I recalled the individual points of my investigation, I argued mentally with the opinions of the examiners, and I clarified my own understandings, intentions, and motivations. I recalled individual actions, programs, lectures, sermons, statements. Drawing on my unusual memory, I was able, without outside assistance, to clarify my case anew as follows:

"I am hailed before the court, because I follow the concept of a Lutheran pastor, his mission, and that of the church differently from that of the state. I understand the church as the institution of Christ and the pastor as Christ's servant. The substance of that ministry is the Gospel of Jesus Christ. That is the good news God has for the entire world, for every person in every age. That message committed to the church by her Lord contains the bliss of salvation and the damnation of unbelief. The Gospel is necessary to govern and direct the individual's intentions, thoughts, actions, and conscience. After a person's faults and inadequacies are exposed, the Gospel is needed to cure, correct, and remove those problems. The life of an individual as well as that of all humanity has a tendency to rise or fall depending on whether it draws closer to or moves farther away from the Gospel. All depends on the genuineness of one's relationship to Christ. Mere formality in this respect is condemned. 'Not everyone who says to me, "Lord, Lord," will enter the kingdom of heaven' [Matt. 7:21].

"As I examine congregational practice and the everyday life of parishioners and compare it with the life of the godless, I find many positive values among believers, but also much lack of love, trust, and obedience to the Lord. The church's duty is to proclaim the Gospel, which alone can reform people and all their relationships at all times. I too must stand here before the court as one called by the holy Gospel. As a person, I too can err, doubt, and fall. But I have a duty and, thank God, also the possibility of returning to my Lord by means of the Gospel, to receive his love and mercy anew, and to interpret it to all people, and also here in court. God calls no one to a mission of evil and wickedness, which are wrong—*sin*—but from which, thankfully, there is redemption, an escape, another chance because of Jesus Christ."

Today it is difficult for me to reconstruct my train of thought 25 years ago. Then I was definitely more flexible and sharper than I am today. That keenness, however, accounted for many of my mistakes and faults and opened me up to dangers other people did not notice. Generally, a quick mind is an indifferent life companion. As a case in point, when I was mentally preparing my defense, I revealed very little of the exercise to my fellow-detainees.

I did, however, play the role of prosecutor in preparing my cellmate Pecho for his upcoming trial. I played the role to the hilt, hoping to prepare him for the sharpest arguments a prosecutor might unleash against him. In a short time, Pecho was so upset trying to match his defense to the tactics of the prosecution that he asked me to stop.

When I met Pecho later in Leopoldov [penitentiary]—his case came up before mine—he told me that his trial was worse than our roleplay. Poor fellow, he was sentenced to 22 years.

The sharp mind can be abused. It is capable of mercilessly treating ideas, things, and people, and is even able to kill. It needs the love of the Gospel, the hope of the Gospel, and the living Christ in order to keep from driving one to despair or to indifference toward others.

While waiting for our respective trials, we played all kinds of games to rid ourselves of gloomy thoughts. In time we became accomplished players. And yet our mental and emotional state was refreshed and strengthened incomparably more by religious meditation, prayers, Scripture passages, and hymn singing. Those means formed, enlivened, sustained, and reformed a person's character.

The days passed wearily. Summer was coming to an end when I finally received notice of my trial for August 31, 1951. Once again I reviewed my entire case. But by this time it had become a farce in my mind. It seemed funny to me that a case such as mine should be brought up before a state court, that the law of the land would busy itself with such "accusations."

If my case was scarcely worth presenting before a court, my appearance was even less presentable. The tattered grey clothes I had worn to my classes had been on me continually since March 14, 1951—day and night. Unpressed, unbrushed, mended here and there by my tailoring skills with an illegally obtained needle and thread, my clothes hung loosely on my 20 kilogram [44 pound] lighter frame as proof of the highly subsidized prison care. My shirt was the same one I had when I was arrested: knitted, pale blue, without a tie.

An attempt was made to make me more presentable. The day before the trial I was given a shave and a haircut. Even so I was a pitiful case. For lack of a mirror I had no idea how I looked, but I did get a glimpse of myself in one along the narrow corridor to the Palace of Justice. Total strangers looked at me with surprise and pity as the guard led me to the courtroom.

I have no idea who told my church members and my family the date of the trial. It could only have been one of my sympathetic guards. At any rate, my family and parishioners were already gathered outside the judgment hall. Some of them gasped audibly, and some sobbed when they saw me.

The guard led me directly to the defendant's bench, seated me, and sat down next to me. On the way he had cautioned me not to look around, nor greet anyone, nor speak to anyone, and that I must obey his gestures.

I noticed out of the corner of my eye that more than 20 of my parishioners were present, besides some people I did not know. Among the spectators was Dr. Ladislav Lanštiak, the mission consultant of the church, representing the bishop general's office in Bratislava. The guard chided me when I glanced to the side.

The hubbub in the courtroom bothered me. After a period of suspense, the panel of judges entered the hall with Presiding Judge Jozef Pavelka. He was appointed from the ranks of the people, from a workers' cadre. Lacking any required legal training, he was simply there to "perform the will of the people." I cannot say he was malicious, but rather ignorant. He could not comprehend the intricacies of the case. He only knew that he was to render a judgment according to instructions. But whose? Probably the panel's, whose judgment I was never given to read.

13

The Trial Begins

The entire courtroom rose to its feet—as did I—to greet the panel of judges. The trial was finally ready to begin.

After constituting the court proceedings, procurator Dr. Pavel Winter took the floor. Out of the convoluted investigators' report, he prepared the criminal charges against me, namely, the abuse of the religious functions stated in Par. 123 of the first penal code, #86/50, according to which I was accused of the following transgressions:

a. that for an indefinite period of time I was training youth anti-socialistically;

b. that on an indeterminate date I loaned my pupil, Ján Hudak, books that were written in an anti-progressive spirit;

c. that I disputed the Marxist world-view in religion classes;

d. that I called working people "dogs";

e. that on February 11, 1951, as a Lutheran pastor in a sermon in the Háj church, I preached in the presence of the Czechoslovak Youth League (ČSM) that they were thieves who had come to report the sermon.

In effect, I was charged with abusing my spiritual activities and my religion classes with the intention of exerting an influence in political matters unfavorable to the people's democratic system in the republic.

After the reading of the accusation came the testimony. The prosecution called its first witness, Štefan Kováč, who was to confirm all the items of my indictment. When the presiding judge announced the witness and introduced him, I was surprised that I did not know him. When the judge asked the witness if he knew me, he replied honestly that he did not know me and that he had never seen me before. The entire courtroom felt that a kind of fraud had been perpetrated. The prosecutor was taken aback, and so was the panel.

What had happened was that the ŠTB had brought in the wrong Štefan Kováč. There was nothing left for the president but to postpone the trial indefinitely until the right witness could be found.

The guard hustled me out of the courtroom and would not permit me to talk to anyone or even to look around. Only after my departure from the hall did the others disperse.

So I had to wait in my cell again until I was told when the next hearing would be held. I was informed about it some eight weeks later: the trial was reset for November 2, 1951.

Once again the prescribed formalities were conducted. Once again I was given strict instructions. And once again my family and parishioners were present, as was Bishop Chabada's representative, Ladislav Lanštiak. I could tell the proceedings moved him deeply, for he wept through the trial. He must have reported to the bishop that every Lutheran pastor was in danger of being similarly tried and condemned.

Following the formalities, the prosecutor repeated the same accusations. When I was allowed to speak, I defended myself with the arguments I had rehearsed mentally. I could not control myself during the prosecutor's cunning and false accusation, "that I called the working people dogs." I jumped off the bench and standing before the judges I defended myself vehemently.

"What do you think? Are you saying that I consider my parents, my brothers and sisters, and my parishioners 'dogs?' They are all working people. I was simply quoting the saying, 'It doesn't hurt the moon when the dogs bark at it.' One cannot interpret those words allegorically, as though someone were a dog and someone else were the moon. The saying simply means that it is futile to fight God. Parables can be interpreted not only allegorically but also typologically and figuratively."

At my outburst, President Pavelka removed this point from the record. The trial resumed with the calling of witnesses. This time the right Štefan Kováč appeared, together with Ján Hudak.

Štefan Kováč uttered a bald-faced lie, that the representatives of the ČSM announced to me beforehand that they were going to attend the church service on February 11, 1951, that I recognized them and preached that they were thieves.

In his testimony, the other witness, Ján Hudak, denied Kováč's testimony of my awareness of the ČSM members in the church service, nor did he interpret my sermon as an attack upon their organization. As for the books I loaned him, he said he had asked me for them, and that I had warned him not to lend them to anyone else. He didn't say a word against me, not even when I requested permission of the presiding judge to cross-examine the witnesses.

When I confronted the contradictory testimony of witnesses Ko-váč and Hudak, the prosecutor jumped up with a shout, reminding me that I was the defendant in the case and for that reason had no right to pose such questions. The president obviously had deprived me of any defense by not objecting to the prosecutor's silencing of me. And, even though the witnesses disagreed and Hudak's testimony denied and contradicted that of Kováč, the court accepted Kováč's testimony.

In his remarks, the prosecutor faulted me, saying that while the rest of the pastors had accommodated themselves to Marxist doctrine, I had not, but that I had instead sharply set the Christian position over against the Marxist.

At that I requested permission to ask the prosecutor a question.

"Mr. Prosecutor, are you identifying your materialistic world-view with my Christian view?"

He replied, "No, I am not."

"Then neither do I identify my Christian world-view with your Marxist one. So we are agreed on this one point. Why then are you judging me?"

I got no reply and was effectively silenced from any further cross examination of the witnesses.

To the court secretary's credit, I must say she entered Hudak's testimony correctly, and, I believe, my defense as well.

In his summation, the prosecutor did not fail to make an issue of his impression that I was very shrewd and talented, and that I was able to defend myself against any charge. He regarded this as a negative point for me and demanded a correspondingly heavier penalty for me.

Throughout the proceedings my court-appointed defender spoke up for me only twice. The first time, he requested the president of the panel to admit the testimony of one of my parishioners, a woman who wished to testify about my work and sermons—a request the president summarily rejected, since the testimony would have supported my case.

The second time, in his summary of the proceedings, he said, "We see that the defendant is very guilty. However, I would ask the court to consider the social origins of the defendant and the fact that he has no previous criminal record."

I do not care to repeat how I defended myself. I will only summarize from my closing statement, which I believe lasted almost half an hour.

I mentioned my parents, poor farmers, and my hard life with seven siblings in the family; how I acquired a higher education by my own efforts; how I worked enthusiastically in the church; of my participation in the Slovak National Uprising (SNP) against the Nazi occupation in World War II; of the vital mission of the church in society; and of the need for brotherhood among people.

Further, I pointed out that the present state of our society reveals a conflict between faith and unbelief, between Christ and Anti-Christ, between religion and atheism, between the Bible and Marxism.

I continued, "I have done nothing beyond the normal duties of an Evangelical pastor of the Augsburg Confession, and my church administration has never in any way advised me to depart from the [Lutheran] Church's doctrine and practice. On the contrary, it has praised my work as exemplary.

"The federal constitution guarantees us freedom of religion. Neither the Bible nor the church are banned in this country, and so it is impossible to judge me for my pastoral activity, which is in harmony with the Bible, the charter of the church, and the constitution of the state. As a believing Christian, I am aware of my failings, and I therefore regret every word and every act by which I have deviated from the ideals of God's kingdom, and I beg the mercy of God. And I beg you, honorable court, for a just decision."

14

The Verdict and Sentence

The silence in the courtroom was almost palpable. The president left the room to confer with the panel. When they returned in a short time, Presiding Judge Pavelka read the verdict (which, incidentally, was never delivered to me) that the state court judged me guilty of the criminal offense of misusing my religious functions according to Art. 123 of Statute 86/50(Zb), and sentenced me to the loss of liberty for two years and ten months, the confiscation of all my property, a fine of 20,000 crowns (which, if not payable, would increase my sentence by two months), and the loss of civil rights for an additional five years after the prison term.

This was followed by the reasons for the verdict:

a. for lending to J. Hudak (and thereby circulating) books written in an anti-progressive spirit;

b. for claiming in a religion class on June 26, 1951 (actually it was the 27th), that religion is persecuted in our country; and

c. for preaching on February 2, 1951, as a Lutheran pastor, in the Háj church in the presence of members of the ČSM: "Brothers and sisters, we see that the church has become a trap, into which thieves come to catch us in our words in order to bring charges against us."

In essence, I was judged guilty of misusing the performance of my spiritual duties and related functions with the intention of exerting a negative influence on political life unfavorable to the people's democratic system of the republic.

At the conclusion of the charges, the president of the panel asked me and the prosecutor, "Are you satisfied with the verdict?"

I stated my dissatisfaction, and appealed the verdict at once.

The defender asked me if I was serious about appealing the verdict, and I asked him in turn, "What do I have to lose?" He agreed that I indeed had nothing to lose and said that he would prepare an appeal and submit it to the supreme court.

The prosecutor was satisfied with the verdict and said he would not appeal it.

Thereupon the guard led me out of the courtroom. He did not permit me to speak to anyone, nor even to cast a parting glance at anyone. When my brother hurried after me to give me an apple, he was not allowed to do even that.

I didn't have a watch, but I believe the proceedings lasted from 9 A.M. until 3 P.M.

In the cell, my fellow-prisoners were waiting for me anxiously. My lunch had gotten cold on the table, but I did not pause to eat until I had informed my neighbors by Morse code about the outcome of my trial. Then I ate my meal and discussed with my cellmates Kudašík and Slimák the course of the trial and my impressions of it. The recital brought tears to their eyes. I myself did not feel like crying. I took this also as a duty to be performed in the service of the Lord.

I knew that after the judgment I would be taken from the state prison in Bratislava to another for the serving of the sentence. I had no idea where that would be, but I decided to prepare my fellow prisoners for my departure by beginning to teach them the Morse code, so they would not be completely forsaken when I left. Kudašík had given up on the instruction earlier, insisting he could never learn it, and so I continued with Slimák. He had learned only a portion of the method when, suddenly on November 9, 1951—obviously without forewarning—I was taken to Leopoldov.

15

The Sentence Begins

It was an unpleasant, raw autumn day. From my cell I was led down to a walk in front of the prison headquarters, and there eight or ten of us were assembled. We were herded into a "Green Anton" and driven off. I had no idea where they were taking us, but some of my fellow-passengers knew we were headed for Leopoldov.

We did indeed come to Leopoldov, where we prisoners were admitted with a great deal of ceremony. After a long time, we were led through many yards, buildings, and walks to our individual cells. There they removed our civilian clothes and placed all our possessions in a storeroom.

For the first time in prison, I came in contact with the "underground." The hall guard, who came from Košice, asked me in a whisper who I was, why I was imprisoned, and for how long. When I answered him sketchily and he learned that I was a Lutheran pastor, he asked me if I wanted any of my belongings smuggled into my cell. I asked him what he meant.

"Well," he said, "a comb, cigarettes, matches, food, money..."

At the time I had nothing but a comb. I was truly as poor as a church mouse.

When one of my fellow inmates heard of the offer, he told me to ask the guard to smuggle him some cigarettes, cookies, a jar of plum butter, and other items. I did, and the guard brought all the things via a different corridor to the room where we were issued our prison uniforms. We had to walk totally naked through the warden's office to the room where we put on our prison garb.

By the special favor of our friendly guard I got some decent clothes and boots, and, of course, a comb, while my fellow inmate got his cigarettes, cookies, and plum butter.

After we were dressed, our names were entered in the prison register. Then they squeezed four of us into a solitary confinement cell. Four straw mattresses practically filled the entire floor, with just enough space in one corner for a pail to accommodate our lesser or greater "needs." The room was on the ground floor, with a window facing the yard. Unventilated, it was stifling and reeked of excrement. The odor increased every time the pail was used. It was left in the room unemptied and unrinsed for several weeks. Whenever it was disturbed, it emitted a horrible stench.

Into that setting the guard brought us our supper. We had missed lunch that day. The guard paid unusual attention to me, choosing me to help divide the food. I welcomed the opportunity to step out of the stinking cell into the corridor for a few minutes, especially since the window could not be opened. Add to that inconvenience the fact that the room was unheated, even though it was already November. All in all, the cell was a disgusting introduction to my prison sentence.

The first night I prayed aloud and sang a few sacred hymns. The next day, my cellmates asked me to pray and sing hymns. Interestingly, the inmate who made the request was a Roman Catholic and a Communist party member. I don't remember his name. The only names I recall are those of Chudovský, a Lutheran from somewhere in Liptov County, and Grešo from Bratislava.

Prayers and meditations were generally very much desired and proved very helpful in counteracting depression. For me, on the other hand, it was a bitter experience to note how spiritually immature and untrained these people were. They expected and needed spiritual comfort, but they did not know how to comfort themselves, and even less to offer spiritual consolation and encouragement to others. They were typical consumers of spiritual values, but not at all producers and suppliers of them.

The second or third day, an ŠTB agent came to our cell periodically to verify all kinds of statistics and to ask us if we wanted to work. I volunteered to go to work in a mine. We were taken to be photographed for some kind of record. Other prisoners did the photographing. Our photographer was a former first lieutenant, whose wife was the daughter of a confectioner, who was also a prisoner in Leopoldov. We got acquainted in no time.

Then we were given a questionnaire to fill out. This was conducted by another prisoner, Dr. Riesz, a former professor from Banská Štiavnica. In reviewing my completed questionnaire, he amused me by noting, "Finally one Lutheran pastor! Until now the only ones suffering here are Roman Catholic priests." He intended his remark as praise for the priests.

I replied quickly, "Consider why the priests are being imprisoned. I am here only because of my religious convictions."

Many of the Catholics were sentenced for political and even criminal offenses as former members of the Hlinka People's Party, the Hlinka Guard, for appropriating church property and engaging in anti-state activities.

Dr. Riesz was one such. He suddenly lost his self-confidence and stopped acting superior. He informed me that my application for the mines had been considered and that a decision had been made. I would not go into the mines. Evidently I was a "beneficiary" of a network the Catholic priests had formed in Leopoldov. They identified, searched for, and followed their political opponents among the prisoners and plotted against them. Dr. Martin Straško, J. Lichner, and J. Ursíni could provide many details of these intrigues.

Riesz informed me that I would be going to a mattress manufacturing department, and that it was already arranged that I would be in the same workroom with M. Straško and J. Lichner. Five or six days later I actually was taken to the "mattressers" room where the aforementioned men were.

There were as many as 44 of us assigned to the mattress shop. The room was furnished with beds as well as straw mattresses on the floor. I was given a straw mattress next to J. Lichner, who was a church member of mine, but was also a well-known official in the Czecho-Slovak government-in-exile in London [during WW II].

There I began to become accustomed to the life of a prisoner serving out a sentence. In general I must admit that doing one's time is incomparably more pleasant, convenient, and tolerable than being in detention for investigation. The prison sentence is prescribed with certain rules and some kind of order, whereas during the investigation one is totally subject to the whim and will of the interrogators, who are a law unto themselves.

My first meeting with Lichner and Straško took place in the mattress factory. The guard took me there by myself, leading me between long rows of work benches, behind which the mattress makers labored. There was no introduction of the "new worker" to the others. The guard took me to an empty table at the end of the workroom, and gave me my tools: a regulator, a crooked needle, a straight needle, twine, and a thickly stuffed mattress, which had to be sown and aligned to match the cover to the back.

My instructor was M. Straško, a mattress finisher. I had not known Martin before this, though he had heard of me soon after I arrived in Leopoldov. Captain J. Pecho, with whom I had spent some time in the state prison, had told him about me.

When I met Lichner, we were both surprised. At home he had been a large man, half a head taller than I, and weighing about 120 kilograms [264 pounds]. Now he was thin and bony, with a sunken face and glasses that slipped off the end of his protruding nose. He greeted me with glistening eyes and a rasping voice. He said I too had lost weight. (I was indeed emaciated, weighing less than 62 kilograms [137 pounds].) And yet I was still quite hale and hearty.

Though Lichner and Straško told me very little about themselves, they were curious about me. I held back no secrets, but told them everything about myself, the investigation, and the trial. They wanted to know what had happened prior to my detention, because Lichner was arrested two years before I was. He was amazed at my broad knowledge of the imprisoned officers, whom I knew only from our coded messages in the Bratislava detention center.

They in turn informed me about conditions in Leopoldov, of the Guardist and Hlinka cliques among the prisoners, how presumptuous they were even here, how they assumed and held key positions in the prison hierarchy, how the guards granted them favors, how they were able to manipulate vulnerable prisoners, how they tried to kill Ursíni with a brick thrown from a wall, and how they dominated the Sunday cultural programs.

At the time the prisoners were able to meet in a hall for cultural endeavors, which they themselves planned under the supervision of the ŠTB and conducted with participants it provided. Often a German officer named Tiele entertained as a violinist. I myself attended the gatherings only three times, and then only as a spectator. I only went because it gave me an opportunity to meet with fellow inmates whom I could not otherwise meet. Some 200–300 prisoners gathered for the occasions.

My two friends had met other inmates during their terms in Leopoldov. They warned me against the dangerous ones and recommended for special attention those who needed my incidental advice and support. In all sincerity, they displayed true concern for me personally. When they noticed that I was weak or thin, they fed me as well as they could. With the help of sympathetic guards, they got me double portions for lunch and supper.

At first my stomach could not tolerate the extra amounts, but as I became used to them, Straško was amazed at how much I was able to eat. Neither he nor Lichner had such an appetite. In four weeks I gained 15 kilograms [43 pounds].

In my relations with the other prisoners, I was able to earn the respect of many of them by my behavior and work, and especially by the knowledge I revealed in debates. And there was a lot of debating going on, on every imaginable subject. I soon got a reputation as a ready and tenacious debater.

Lichner encouraged me to debate in order to influence especially the younger non-clerical Catholic inmates, whom the priests were trying to gain for their Hlinka political camp. These politicized clergy looked bigotedly at non-Catholics as traitors to the Slovak nation. I was seen as bringing to the prison an entirely different spirit: a freer and nobler attitude without provoking animosity.

I had gained such sincere respect from many prisoners that I was selected unanimously—even by the Roman Catholic clergy— to be the festival speaker at the Christmas Eve program.

I spoke about love according to 1 John 4, without resorting to cheap emotionalism. In comforting and reverent words I said that Christmas brings a message of love, that Christmas is indeed only about God's love toward the human race, and its meaning and blessing is understood only by the one who lives in love. That love must be patient as well as humble, not boastful but committed, trusting, and enduring. As tenderly as possible, I touched upon our plight, our separation from our families, and our suffering.

This was followed by our holiday "dinner"—truly festive and disproportionately richer than usual. We even had fried fish. I myself had been in the kitchen several days to help fry the fish, and was always able to bring a few pieces back to our cell. The cooks gladly shared the food, and the guards had no inkling of the favor.

For my closest friends I was able to withdraw several hundred crowns from my account. I could do this because my funds were sent along with me to Leopoldov. And because the sentence was not yet served and my appeal not yet filed, the director of the prison permitted me to draw on my account.

16

A Close Call

That Christmas celebration, however, was the last in Leopoldov. Already on December 26, 1951, the majority of us were transferred to Ilava [prison]. Leopoldov was reserved only for the more prominent and politically important prisoners with longer sentences.

The facilities at Leopoldov were remodeled to accommodate that class of prisoner. For several weeks I myself worked on the project. We demolished old earthworks and underground passageways. The work took place in December. Although we suffered from the cold, it was healthier work than in the mattress factory, despite the fact that I returned to my room bone tired. As a bonus, we were able to round up extra food: raw cabbage or carrots that had been stored away, or cooked potatoes intended for the swine.

Also working among our "domestic resources" was another Turčan [a man from the Turiec region], J. Ursíni, a former vice-president of the republic, and Michalík, the director of the National Bank. These men occasionally treated me to the potato cache and even salted them for me. The potatoes were not only good to eat, but they warmed my hands at the same time. Director Michalík even gave me some onions. This really made me happy. In a few days, we liquidated the pigsty like a plundering horde. I'll never forget those stolen moments spent in their company.

Situated above this secret surplus diet source was a concrete wall bordering the pigpen at one corner of the star-shaped Leopoldov fortress. We were working about six meters [almost 20 feet] below ground level, away from close supervision, in an excavation so deep that one could not get to another place from there. I had no trouble bypassing the entire job site.

Still comparatively young, I could climb to the top of the wall and walk from one end to the other. This was not a special athletic accomplishment, but it did provide some amusement in an otherwise boring day. Since it was easy to become dizzy atop the wall, one had to concentrate on one's footing.

On the other side of the wall there was freedom. One could see the road leading from town to the fortress, and people on the road, no doubt coming to visit prisoners. Now and then we would wave at them on the sly. I did too. But we had no hidden intentions. We didn't know the people we were waving at.

One time, about an hour after I had waved to someone on the road, an ŠTB came looking for me. It didn't take him long to trace me through the guards to find me at the job site. When he located me, he asked if I had been working steadily since morning. The guard, out of whose sight we had worked most of the time, assured the secret police that I had indeed been working there the whole morning, and the agent left.

I didn't ascribe any significance to the occasion as we went for lunch to our cells. We had just eaten when the guards locked the cells for the afternoon break. But then, in less than ten minutes, they stuck the key in the door and opened it. Suddenly the room was filled with alarm.

What was happening? "A Filzung," they whispered. [Evidently a German expression derived from Filz, for "louse"; so probably a delousing procedure.]

The supervisor of the room calmed everyone down and restored order.

"Uhorskai, come with me!" the ŠTB barked.

The tension in the room increased. But Martin S. was able to whisper to me, "You're heading for solitary confinement. What can I give you?"

As it was, he didn't have a chance to give me anything. All I could do was grab my cap and go.

The ŠTB took me in the direction of the solitary cells. I was beginning to think Martin was right. We walked down the solitary cell corridor. I was wondering at which door the ŠTB would stop, push me into the cell, and lock it. We passed some ten cells on the right and ten on the left without stopping, then went to another corridor farther on. My anxiety diminished as my curiosity grew as to where I was headed.

My question was answered as we arrived at the administration office. The room was empty. The agent seated me in a chair, told me to wait there, and left. I waited there alone. Shortly the director entered, and I stood up. Again I was told to sit. And then the questioning began.

Name? Why was I sentenced? How long have I been in prison? And so on, running the gamut of banalities.

Suddenly, "Do you know a Miss Hermanska?"

"No."

"Do you know a Miss Horánska?"

"Yes."

"When did you see her last?"

"A long time ago, when I was still free."

"Did you see her today?"

"No."

"How was she dressed?"

"I don't know. But when I saw her in the winter, she wore a leather jacket and a sheepskin cap. In the summer, she favored blue clothes."

"What is this young woman to you?"

"She's a member of my congregation."

"She claims she's your fiancee, that she saw you today on the wall, that you waved to her, and she waved back to you. She came to visit you, and wants to talk to you. If you will admit that you saw her and waved to her, I'll grant her a visit."

"Although I know her well," I tried to explain, "she is not my fiancee—which, however, does not eliminate the possibility that she could be under different circumstances. But I would like to talk to her. If you will make it possible, I will be grateful to you."

"Admit that you saw her."

"I did not see her."

And so the game went on for about half an hour. In the end a guard was ordered to take me back to my cell.

Everyone was still in the ward. The noon break was not yet over. They all stared at me, asking me silently where I had been. When I told them in some detail where I had been, M. Straško burst out with a laugh, "You're really lucky. If that had happened to me, I'd be in solitary by now."

We returned to our jobs shortly, and the guards paid no attention to me whatever.

My fellow workers said that someone certainly had waved from the wall (as I well knew), but no one had betrayed me [by informing the guards] that I was on the wall at all that day. And Horánska was actually in Leopoldov that day, as I learned when I met her upon my release from prison. However, she never did tell me the details of her visit.

The apprehension of the guards and of the director could have been a warning to me to be more watchful. Some two weeks later, six inmates actually escaped from Leopoldov, from the very same demolition project. They had broken through a wall 180 cm [6 feet] thick. Among them was an American employee of the U.S. consulate in Bratislava [John Hvasta]. He was never caught. He had made his way to the American embassy in Prague, where he found sanctuary until the U.S. obtained his release and he returned home.

17

The Next Stop: Ilava

In preparation for our transfer to Ilava [a concentration camp during World War II], we were gathered from multi-prisoner cells and placed in separate cells. A great many of us were scheduled to leave. We took advantage of the opportunity to attach ourselves to our closest acquaintances, so that we could be placed together in the new facilities. For that reason I kept close to Martin Straško, the former pastor from Poltár, and with Jozef Nadeniček, a Bohemian Brethren locksmith from Moravia. While waiting for a long time (I think it was a night and a day), we talked about everything.

It was there that I was sought out by a Roman Catholic priest, Dr. Hatala, a tall, slender man, who appeared to be suffering from tuberculosis, and who died shortly after his release from prison. In our meeting, he was particularly interested in the ecumenical movement and was well-informed on all the ecumenical conferences held in Europe. I was surprised by the interest of the Roman Catholic church in the subject and of Dr. Hatala's interest in particular. There was not as much preoccupation with the subject among us Lutherans.

Our discussion impressed upon me the organizational ability and zeal of Roman Catholicism in following everything taking place in the world of religion. The conscientious Catholic clergy I met in prison were already informed about me, came to me with various religious questions and views, and enjoyed debating with me about all kinds of ecclesiastical matters. They respected my education and my access to doctrinal, ethical, historical, and general religious issues. Our debates/discussions were always on a high level. Very few of them were bound to what they called a "breviary view." There were, of course, some shallow and vacuous clergy in the prison, but I quickly dismissed them.

The time for our transfer to Ilava had arrived.

After we were loaded onto buses, we wondered where we were

going, as we had not been told beforehand. Even though the shades were drawn in the buses, those who knew the country said we were going to Ilava.

We arrived there late in the evening of December 27, 1951, having missed both lunch and supper. It was very cold. I remember young Dr. Sabó, a repatriate from Hungary, who was weak from tuberculosis and shivering from the cold. I gave him my scarf for a little warmth. The poor man had evidently been arrested in the summertime, for we were being transferred in our own civilian clothes. It wasn't until the next day that we were given our prison uniforms.

I was assigned to a cell with my chosen friends, Martin Straško and Jozef Nadeniček. It was a small cell built for solitary confinement. Everyone got one blanket. The small space was taken up by three beds consisting of a metal frame and three boards, without a straw mattress. The floor was concrete. Since we could not all sleep on the cots at the same time, we spent the first night on the cement floor in a freezing, unheated cell.

By the second night we had invented a system. We made one large bed out of the three by placing the frames side by side, placing the boards on it, and on it we spread one blanket. Then, lying like three matches in a box, we covered ourselves with two blankets. Obviously, when one of us turned during the night, the other two had to turn also in order to fit on the bed and for all to be covered and protected from the cold. We didn't sleep well, but we slept that way for about three weeks.

During those three weeks, the food was meager—as it was in solitary cells. But our spiritual morale was high, our physical condition respectable, and our sense of humor abundant, with some to spare.

We prayed and meditated regularly, but chiefly we sang sacred songs. And we sang them in full voice. The guards couldn't help but hear us. They peeked through the door window, but made no comments about our singing.

I tried at once to make contact with the neighboring cells by Morse code, but not every cell knew the code. Those who did not asked me verbally to write out the code for them. I wrote it on the bottom of the drinking cups that were passed from cell to cell. In that way our neighbors began to learn it. And so we settled into a regular routine in this aspect of prison life as well.

At best, life was bitter and wretched for those three weeks. Ilava was unprepared to receive and accommodate so many prisoners. Gradually the workshops began operating. We even got some straw for our cell. It was a relief to be able to sleep on a straw mattress at least.

Previously the prisoners got to work in the factory only by the influence of a superior. There [in Ilava], too, favoritism ruled, perhaps even more than elsewhere. In a short time I was assigned to the mattress factory with Straško. Nadeniček joined the locksmiths as a mechanic. Even though we were separated, we did get to see each other on our walks, and we occasionally spent some time together.

18

The Ongoing Lutheran/ Catholic Prison Dialog

In the mattress shop, the old acquaintances were joined by a few new faces; and the atmosphere of mistrust increased accordingly. I knew very few of the prisoners there. Straško and I were the only Lutheran pastors in the shop. Martin had little confidence in the Roman Catholic clergy, and his argumentative nature didn't help his relations with them.

On the other hand, I got along quite well with them and they with me. I noticed many eyes fixed on me at work and knew that they were talking about me. Clearly their comments must have been favorable, for about the third day in the shop, as we were walking through the room, an elderly, seventyish Dr. Barnáš, a former consecrating bishop from Spiš County, stopped me. He introduced himself to me and said he had heard about me and noticed by my appearance that I was famished. Many of us were weak from the bad accommodations and rations.

He asked me not to refuse his offer—a piece of bread the size of my fist, a whole day's portion. I was surprised by his gift, but I accepted it with thanks and with an apology for not deserving it and for not being able to return the favor. That was not why he gave me the bread, he said. He simply wanted to strike up an acquaintance with me. It was a propitious introduction.

Dr. Barnáš was well-trained in Hebrew and was pleasantly surprised to learn from our Lutheran publications that our General Bishop Čobrda was a member of the commission for translating the Old Testament and had translated the psalms. Until then he had known Čobrda only as a broadly educated person and a good speaker. His comments about our bishop general revealed a broad knowledge of the Lutheran clergy by the Roman Catholic prison network. I discovered that they ranked our Lutheran pastors on various rungs of a ladder. It was interesting to me that they placed me quite high on their scale of evaluation. This became clear to me several weeks later as I was working in the Ilava mattress shop.

Picture a room eight meters long and about three to four meters wide, with work benches down the center. Prisoners sat on opposite sides of the tables, sowing hidden stitches with hooked needles, then finishing the borders with visible stitches made with straight needles. The mattresses were then passed on to others to do the final sewing.

In the workroom, we grouped ourselves in such a way as to choose a congenial partner across the table. Opposite me sat M. Straško, and next to me was the Greek Catholic bishop, Dr. Hopko. We engaged in continuous conversation. I was familiar with the Greek Catholic church and its priests from my personal contacts in Bardejov and in the Prešov diocese.

We talked about theology and history and what not. Straško merely listened, because his remarks were often barbed and contributed little to the discussion. Because of his one-sidedness and, I suspect, also because of his tactlessness, the Catholic priests did not care to debate with him. He seemed to react almost jealously toward me, fearing I would become converted by the Catholic clergy. His attitude struck me as similar to that of an anxious and jealous mother who follows and limits her daughter's associations so that her reputation will not be harmed. I considered Martin's attitude amusing and made nothing of it. Though he was insecure with my independence, he remained my closest friend.

In one of our discussions at the job, Bishop Dr. Hopko made a remark that must have been occupying him for some time.

"Father Uhorskai, you'd make an excellent Catholic priest. You're very disciplined, highly educated, and a deeply dedicated believer. Come over to us. I'd accept you any time. You'd get along very well among us."

Of course, these comments surprised me. Martin's eyes just flashed, but he didn't say a word. He simply stared at me and waited impatiently for my reply.

I answered very calmly: "Reverend Bishop, I think I'll remain a Lutheran pastor, for in my early childhood my mother taught me the hymn, 'Preserve Us, Lord, without Ceasing, in the Augsburg Confession.' [The hymn is a translation by the Slovak hymnologist and hymn writer Samuel Hruškovic, of M. K. Becker's German versification of the Augsburg Confession in a 32-stanza hymn sung to *Erhalt uns, Herr, bei deinem Wort.*]

"Over the course of many years of study and life in the Lutheran Church of the Augsburg Confession, I have become more grounded in this confession; and as you see, it hasn't harmed me but rather strengthened me."

The bishop was somewhat disappointed. But Martin rubbed his hands together with satisfaction, and I believe he would have hugged me for deflecting the bishop's smooth approach. And again our friendship was bonded.

I don't know why Bishop Hopko was interned, but I think he was the victim of the conflict between the Greek Catholic church and the state, which wanted to make them a part of the Orthodox church. Contentions among the two church groups were especially vehement in eastern Slovakia.

These discussions were one of the ways we shortened and made more bearable the time in the dusty and unhealthy atmosphere of the mattress factory. Forty-four of us were housed in one ward to give the guards better control over us. Of these 44, only three were Lutheran pastors [reflecting the ratio of Lutherans to Catholics in Slovakia].

The third member of our Lutheran trio was Juraj Želman, an official from Bratislava, said to be a repatriate from Hungary. He, Straško, and I prayed together and sang hymns every morning and evening. Since I knew many of the hymns from memory, I would line them out and we would then sing them together. Naturally, we were observed. The Roman Catholic clergy also prayed together, some formally, others ex corde, some ostentatiously, others reverently. We respected each other yet observed each other closely. There was no avoiding—nor could there have been—eventual confrontation. Beginning with conversations, we ended often in theological disputes.

Once—I think it was Easter Eve, 1952—we spent two whole days carrying on a dogmatic disputation on Catholic and Lutheran teachings. On the Catholic side were professors, doctors of philosophy, canons, deacons, parish priests, and chaplains—most of them older than I, then 32–33 years old. Those who were younger were more moderate and debated very seriously. The few outbursts from them were quickly suppressed by their more temperate brothers.

On the Lutheran side, I was the sole debater. Želman had less education and training, and Martin could not control his reactions. Nevertheless they were my faithful fans, cheering me when I defended the Lutheran teachings with ready and fitting arguments supported with proofs from Scripture and history.

The outcome of these disputations was a mutual respect and rapprochement, with the result that the Catholic clergy looked upon the SECAV as a church founded on Christ and not on some sectarian departures and obstinacy. I can state here that, even though I was a young Lutheran pastor, the fair-minded Catholic priests and professors, young and old, treated me with respect. Even though some of them were saturated with political Catholicism and severely criticized us Lutherans for our opposition during the Slovak State, many of them understood that politicized Christianity was a thing of the past, that now there remained room only for a *Christ*ian Christianity—interested in proclaiming Christ the Savior to sinners throughout the world; to live by his love and to share his love with all people; to commend oneself to the will of God; to accept one's call, justification, and sanctification from God; and to live in the Kingdom of God in peace and in the joy of the Holy Spirit.

Only such Christians, I contended, would gain the respect of the world, even the hostile world, the godless world, the wise world, the highly technical world, those to whom convincing arguments and opinions, speeches and propaganda, are not attractive—but only Christ, the actual way, the actual truth, and the actual life. Today the church is no longer the wisest, the most educated, and the strongest socially and politically. Today the church must be a lover and confessor of God, struggling to get the whole world to accept God's love and God's holiness, God's order and God's peace, God's blessing and God's salvation.

Christ is among us as one who serves the church, and the church only serves the world in his stead. This is not easy for the church. But being a disciple and follower of Christ has never been easy; it has always been a matter of life and salvation. Those who are not concerned about life and salvation are not Christ's disciples. Today we must take Christ seriously—or not at all. This is the view of the church from our human perspective.

From the Lord's perspective, the way is clear. He can create sons for Abraham out of stones. He loved and still loves the world so that those who believe in his Son may not perish but have everlasting life (John 3:16). Man may accept or refuse God's proffered grace.

Even though some of these thoughts were strange to the Catholic clergy and seemed like a harangue, nevertheless the fact that I pressed the points so insistently gained their serious attention and respect. Only in empty political hearts and heads did I call forth unconcealed rejection.

19

Time Out for the Appeal

In describing our coexistence and internal life in Ilava, I have skipped over an important event in my prison experience: the hearing of my appeal before the Supreme court in Prague.

Upon hearing the verdict of the state court in Bratislava, I appealed the judgment. There was only one recourse left: the highest court in the republic. From impressions I received in Leopoldov and Ilava, I didn't expect a drastic change in the verdict. But considering the seriousness of the supreme court of the land, I did tend to expect a fair concern for the case in general. My appearance before the court in Prague was scheduled for January 30, 1952.

The morning of January 25, 1952, I was awakened at 5 A.M. and led to the uniform dispensary, where I was issued a new winter prison outfit. Presumably, it was necessary to represent the prison and its prisoners properly both at the highest court and for the trip there.

Two of us traveled to Prague that day: a Greek Catholic priest (Hricov) and I. Hricov was more than 70 and very frail. He was afraid to make the trip in the bitter and icy weather.

We were escorted by the National Security/Police officers (ZNB) and handed over to the ŠTB. They first took our papers and then confronted us with more documents.

Chief Warden Dobrovodský, a native of Vrbov, addressed us—and especially me—very seriously.

"I've read your dossier and should handcuff you," he said, showing us the cuffs. "But since you are clergy, I assume you will behave reasonably, and I won't have to use them. I happen to be a Lutheran, too."

He then put the handcuffs in a bag and turned us over to a younger colleague.

The trip was hard, slippery, and dangerous, especially the road from the prison to the square, then down the stairs to the train station. Poor old Hricov could hardly walk and was always on the verge of falling. I asked if I could give him a hand, which they let me do when the escort noticed how he was shuffling.

At the station we boarded a separate train and rode to Púchov, where we were to transfer to the express to Prague. While waiting there, the ZNB encountered some problems with the people in the waiting room, who stopped and whispered, "Aha! They're taking the pastors to court!"

I don't know how they guessed we were clergymen—perhaps from our appearance and behavior. They wanted to offer us apples, croissants, bread, and other refreshments. But the ZNB would not allow it. I whispered to my guard that it had been a long time since we had an apple or even a roll. He said civilians weren't allowed to give us anything, but he ran off and brought back half a kilogram of apples and two croissants. Then he asked the station-master to vacate a waiting room for us, which he did at once.

When the express train arrived, we were surprised to have a separate reserved compartment. We were seated comfortably with ZNB guards beside us. Hricov was completely exhausted. One could expect that at his age and in his physical condition. On the contrary, I felt relaxed and much better than in prison. I initiated a conversation with the chief guard, and we covered a wide range of subjects.

When we came to Hranice, a surge of passengers filled the aisle to capacity. Among them was an army captain, who asked our guard if he could sit in our compartment. Permission was readily granted since he was in the army and therefore dependable. Now the discussion became more lively.

The ZNB agents as well as the officer were curious as to how we were treated in prison and in the interrogations. Gratefully and with a touch of gallows-humor I willingly described my experiences in the process. They were pleased to hear of concrete instances in which the interrogated prisoners proved to be morally superior to the ŠTBs, how they led them into ridiculous positions and toyed with them. It was evident that neither the ZNB agents nor the officer sympathized with the ŠTBs. In fact, the officer was so pleased with my story that he asked the guard if he could treat the prisoners to a beer. And so he did. Even though the train was late, the trip went fast for us.

We arrived in Prague between 10 and 11 at night. The chief

escort hailed a taxi to take us to Pankrác prison. They would not admit us there, and after an interminable negotiation, they sent us to the detention center. By this time it was really late.

The place looked like a holding pen. It was filled with people lying on mattresses on the floor. Here and there, there was a cot; but there was no room for us. I tried to convince the guard that we needed to rest up for our appearance at the supreme court the next morning. But he said it was impossible to find any other place to spend what was left of the night.

It was now about 2 A.M. All we could do was lie down fully clothed on a mattress already occupied by someone else. But sleep was out of the question. Our fellow prisoners asked us where we had been confined and how we had gotten to this place. When I told them we had come from Ilava after a stay in Leopoldov, they were surprised and treated us with greater consideration.

At about 5 A.M. there was an uproar in the room as a Filzung was begun. The guard who admitted us during the night tried vainly to explain that the two of us did not belong with the riff-raff in the room, but it did no good. We had to undress completely. Our clothing and bodies were inspected to see if we were concealing anything illegal.

After the delousing, we got our breakfast—blackish water and a piece of bread. Then our ZNBs took over, and we went to the Supreme Court building on Spalená Street—No. 8, I believe.

At the entrance to the court, I saw some of my parishioners, my brother, brother-in-law, and sister-in-law, but we were not allowed to get together. I was taken to one courtroom, Hricov to another.

My case began around 9 A.M. First came the opening ceremony with the presentation of Dr. Wagner, the presiding judge. Then my charges were read, the verdict of the state court in Bratislava, and my appeal prepared by Dr. Šrobár. Everything was formal.

I was then summoned to present my defense. An unofficial defender was there, but he did not get involved in my case.

I repeated in essence the defense I had made in Bratislava.

"I have committed no criminal act against the law of the land. My teaching in school conformed to the article of the national and federal constitution guaranteeing freedom of religion. On that basis I believed we Christians have the right to confess our faith and to teach it to our children according to the relevant laws.

"Furthermore, I fulfilled the required qualifications of a teacher. Neither in my classes nor in my sermons did I advocate the overthrow of the republic, nor did I carry on any anti-government activity, either open or covert. Any disputing of this fact is the result of forced interpretation of my activity. If there is any conflict between Marxism and the Bible concerning Christian teachings, that is not our fault. So long as the Bible is not outlawed, and so long as the activity of my church is not forbidden, I cannot be judged for my faith, for my teaching of the Christian faith, nor for practicing my religion. If you remove from the charges against me—charges based on the conflict between the Bible and Marxism, the disagreement between religion and materialism—then I stand before you innocent.

"There can be no word at all about anti-government activity. If you condemn me, you can condemn all Lutheran pastors and the entire church. I fought for this Republic in the Slovak National Uprising. I am a lawful citizen of the Czechoslovak Republic, and that is why I am appealing to the supreme court of the nation for a dismissal of the verdict of the Bratislava court."

My appeal went on for more than half an hour.

The government prosecutor—a Czech whose name I did not know—then took the floor. He spoke of my religious stubbornness; that my patriotism ended in 1948; that I did not participate in the February events [marking the Communist takeover] nor in the consolidation thereafter; that I did not assist in the socialization of the country; and that there was therefore no reason why the verdict should be rescinded.

The court retired for deliberation for such a brief time that it was evident the decision had been made beforehand.

Presiding Judge Wagner announced, among other things, "You can see from the words of the defendant that he is very intelligent, highly gifted and educated, politically knowledgeable and mature—and so is very dangerous for society. His criminal offense hovers somewhere between the first and second sections of the cited paragraph of the criminal law. Had the government prosecutor reversed his judgment, the Supreme Court would raise the sentence to five years. However, since the Supreme Court rejects the appeal of the defendant, it affirms the judgment of the Bratislava state court."

And with that everything was finished. There was no further

appeal. The sentence had to be carried out to its completion. I was not at all fooled by the results of the deliberation, nor was I surprised.

The preparation for my return to prison was more favorable than my preparation for solitary confinement. I asked for permission to take advantage of the opportunity to speak to my family and parishioners. The prosecutor granted it, but only to talk to my brother and in-laws, and that for just 10 minutes.

The entire affair was concluded before noon.

I learned that Hricov, the Greek Catholic priest, was dispatched exactly as I had been. His son was there with him—also a former Greek Catholic priest, but working at the time in the Sokolovo coal mines, since his government license had also been taken away. Hricov's ZNB escort told me they could have freed and released him completely, but that he didn't show any interest in that possibility. He allegedly cared to say nothing in the court, taking everything apathetically.

We hurried to the station to get the next return train. My family learned from my guard which train we would be taking, so they traveled on the same one. On the trip I was able to talk to my family, who gave me some fruit, pastry, and a piece of chocolate. I assured them that I would endure the sentence, that not too much of it remained, and that God was, is, and will be with me.

We arrived in Ilava again at night. The food I got on the way and had not eaten I divided among the nearest prisoners. They were mostly curious about the course of the trial. The description of the hearing I gave them was exactly what they had expected.

20

Back to Ilava and the Rest of the Sentence

Once again I had to accustom myself to regular prison life.

However, a change occurred a couple of weeks after I returned. A place happened to open up in the basket shop. Some of the prisoners were transferred to Jachymov [Joachimstal] and had to be replaced. At the time one of my fellow countrymen, Gejza Kelemen, a former captain from the counter-reconnaissance, worked in the basket factory. When he saw how certain Catholic prisoners were getting Roman Catholic priests to work in the department, he suggested to the chief guard that Straško and I be assigned to the same place.

The head guard, Bafalík, didn't even want to hear of Straško, because he had known him from the time he was a pastor in Komárno and had a bad impression of him. He approved of me, however, obtained permission to have me transferred, and placed me in the basket detail.

So it was that my apprenticeship began. In no time I learned the technique of making green wicker baskets. They were ordinary baskets for use on farms.

I was assigned to work with a common thief, a former member of the German army, who had lost his leg in the war. His name was Pavel Vlník—a Lutheran, too, but only a nominal one. Nevertheless, I prayed with him and sang hymns for the short time we were able to spend together.

I developed a closer relationship with Gejza Kelemen, whom I mentioned earlier. His faith grew stronger during his prison stay and under the pressure of the surroundings, especially under the influence of politicized Catholicism. He longed for the pure Gospel, the Lutheran ethic, and Lutheran ideology. But the Lutheran way of life was strange to him, conditioned as he was by his lifelong association with the Catholic church. He did agree, however, with my attitude toward political Catholicism, and we grew to be good friends.

Also together with us in the same room was the former president of the ONV in Martin, Jesenský by name, from a well-known Lutheran family, a teacher by profession. He worked in prison as a bookbinder. Though very poor in health, this man was the spiritually strongest person in our group.

There was one more Lutheran there: Reitmajer Zbyněk, a young nominal Lutheran from the High Tatras.

In contrast to this handful of Lutherans, there were in the same ward and workshop some 40 Roman Catholics, of whom about half were priests. The rest were former officers like Kelemen, Hlinka, and Guardist activists and delegates, imprisoned since 1945. The latter were truly Guardist (militia) rabble, a mixture of robbers and murderers (whose names I could mention), with a conglomeration of characters, opinions, and pretensions.

I have no interest in describing them here except to point out the irony of diverse personalities in the same room: the former police major and ZNB officer, Lach, thrown together with Kováč, the professional thief and burglar of the Tatra resort hotels. How very contradictory were the sanctimonious gushings of the vulgar Guardists and the debates between the administrative apparatus of the Hlinka Party and those who took part in the Slovak National Uprising! They were loud in their denunciation of the Lutheran segment of the Slovak nation for its negative position toward the former Slovak State [1939–1945], their venom fairly pouring out of them. They did not refrain from insults, fights, and even death threats. It's something I do not care to dwell on except to mention it as a factor in our particular national experience.

Before long the officers left for Jachymov. Those of us who were left in the basket-weaving shop were a much friendlier group. There were fewer stressful situations and more serious discussions. Among the remaining prisoners, I remember a number of sincere people: Major Sestak, Lieutenant Levák, and Eng. Černok. Many of them were deeply religious and worthy people.

One name lingers in my memory: Dr. L. Aranya from Rožňava, a professor of Slovak at the Hungarian *Gymnázium,* a staunch Hungarian and an equally staunch Catholic. He had been arrested for

Hungarian irredentism [advocating the acquisition of a region included in the boundaries of another country]. The party spread from Košice through the Moldau River valley, through Rožňava, Šafárikovo, Rimavská Sobota, Lučenec, Sahy, Komárno, and all the way to Bratislava. In reality, the movement was plotting a conspiracy against the Czechoslovak Republic.

Aranya was highly educated, and we were able to debate intelligently about philosophy, literature, and history. He also played a good game of chess. Though he was not a Guardist, nor did he agree with them, he remained a bigoted Catholic and Hungarian. Yet he was intellectually above the ignorant attacks of former Hlinka Party members against us Lutherans and chiefly against me. On those occasions, he respected my prudent stand.

After a number of such vicious attacks, I quoted a hymn by Kristina Royová, "Who Will Strengthen Me for the Journey to That Distant Realm of Bliss?" Aranya was captivated by its earnestness and depth.

We got into open disagreement about World War I, the disintegration of the Austro-Hungarian monarchy, and the creation of the countries that replaced it: Czechoslovakia, Yugoslavia, Romania, Bulgaria, Hungary, and Austria. I valued the peaceful establishment of the Czechoslovak Republic and the contributions of France, the USA, and England to its formation. This was unbearable to him. He broke out in uncontrollable anger, after which we didn't speak for nearly two weeks. Later we forgot the matter, and our relationship improved.

21

Carrying on a Prison Ministry

I must mention my relationship also to the older farmers, kulaks, who refused to join the Union of Agricultural Workers (JRD). Among them were some very old men: 85-year-old Čabadaj; 72-year-old Kuricina; Mozeš, also in his 70s; Lisy, the barber; and others. Although they were Roman Catholics, they sided with me and confided their problems and worries to me. When I was doing some dirty domestic work, they would come to me and insist on doing the tasks they considered beneath my station and dignity. In return I found ways to serve them by writing appeals for them for a change in conditions, letters home, and all kinds of pertinent advice.

I was able to provide pastoral counseling for prisoners whose wives at home were unfaithful to them, and I wrote letters to the women at home who were no longer faithful and either sought or were tempted by other men. I also counseled young men whose wives were initiating divorce proceedings because their husbands were in prison or because they disagreed with their spouse's political convictions. My situation presented me with rich possibilities for spiritual activity.

In the meantime, I became the technical manager of the basket workshop. I was then the only Lutheran in the shop. The head warden was a devout Roman Catholic, who was still a member of the Prison Guard Association. Instead of selecting one of the many Catholic priests and professors for the position, he chose me as his confidante, as he told me, for my forthrightness, industriousness, education, and character.

He personally certified my documents in the office and was dismayed that my verdict was not with my court papers. He concluded that my verdict must have some special importance, because it was not shared with me.

By the time I was made the technical supervisor of the basket works, I was already weaving an advanced Dutch [Holland] type of basket. In addition to filling my personal quota, I was responsible for supervising the workers in the shop, delivering additional portions of food to the hardest workers, bringing medicines to the sick, taking patients to the infirmary, receiving materials for the baskets, and expediting the shipment of the finished product.

Although my duties had increased greatly, they served to widen my contacts with the other prisoners. I am amazed at how many I was able to seek out, visit, and comfort—opportunities that would have been impossible otherwise. Every evening I would read and write far into the night and long after the evening mealtime, for the lights were left on while we slept.

During the day I would distribute religious meditations, prayers, and hymns to our fellow-Lutherans in the prison, in the infirmary, and in various departments. During the Easter season I wrote communion prayers and intercessions, composed numerous liturgies for the Lord's Supper, together with absolution, and distributed them to our communicants.

I even administered Holy Communion. I had obtained wafers through the prison network, and the warden provided me with wine. I served the Sacrament in the X-ray room of the infirmary under the most trying circumstances. Yet I was able to administer it successfully and with blessing, even though the ŠTB often banged on the walls to disrupt our worship.

Although the service delayed my infirmary visits, I still had time left over for my regular duties in the hospital and warehouse. My director worried about my getting caught when I left to serve the Sacrament, for that would be bad for him. I told him not to worry if I was a little late on my rounds. As it was, I did not get caught, and he was spared any implication in my activity.

While my director supported me, others were not so friendly. A certain murderer by the name of Klempa from Záhorie was assigned to our room. He was in jail for killing a 10- or 12-year old boy, whom he had first menaced with a knife. This prisoner turned out to be a plant. He reported me to the authorities for reading and writing something at night. The ŠTBs ransacked my room a number of times while we were in the workshop. They rummaged through my bed and closet, but never found anything. I had managed to

115

hide my forbidden books, my Slovak Lutheran hymnal (*Tranoscius*), the Hungarian New Testament, and German Bible in various places: under the table top, the stovepipe, the ventilator in the toilet, the straw mattress, and elsewhere.

Usually, the killers and robbers among us were chosen to spy on and report other prisoners. So I discovered that Danek was one such plant. Often gone for one or two days, he never told us where he was going or where he had been when he returned late.

Another one was "Jožko" [Jozef] Volek, who was somewhat more honest, but who couldn't hide his secret mission. When he returned once after a brief absence, he was very sad and nearly out of his mind. Because I had done him a favor by writing a request for a new trial, he confessed to me in a whisper what he was doing and what he was expected to do.

In the prison administrator's office, a younger officer challenged him, saying, "Jožko, you've killed only one person, but these priests, professors, engineers, and the rest of the gang would get rid of all of us if they had the chance. So report to us what they are saying among themselves. Tell us what kind of people they are, and we'll reduce your sentence by a half."

He was subjected to all kinds of pressure from above. When I asked him what he answered, he told me, "Nothing. How could I squeal on you?"

Whether he tattled on anyone else, I don't know. At any rate, I had no trouble from him.

Jožko Volek was an unusual person—a murderer, yes, but not a killer. He had murdered a man who had insulted and belittled him, who threatened to beat and even kill him, who had already beaten Jožko's mother.

22

The Church
and Totalitarianism

There were a great many Roman Catholic religious in the prison. I would estimate their number between 600 and 700, reflecting their percentage of the religious population of Slovakia. Besides priests, they included nuns, monks, lay brothers, and seminarians.

As I mentioned before, we engaged in numerous conversations, which revealed both their expertise in many areas as well as their prejudices toward us Lutherans. I must admit that I knew less about them and about the internal organization and life of the Roman Catholic church than some of their scholars knew about our Evangelical Church of the Augsburg Confession.

If any of them thought of converting me to Catholicism, they were disappointed. I think I convinced them that I was a genuine Lutheran and that my roots were too deep to allow me to be drawn into a cheap and shallow conversion.

In all of our conversations and debates, I never spoke offensively against the Roman Catholic church and its clergy, which does not mean that I concealed my differing and critical stance. Rather than keeping silent about my convictions, I presented them politely and calmly with appropriate Biblical, dogmatic, and historical reasoning.

From their side, many if not most looked down on Lutheran pastors and considered them to be spiritually shallow, playing a kind of spiritual game—faddish, lacking spiritual and moral stability and firmness, and deficient in learning and responsibility. They saw Lutheran clergy as unripened, unfermented youth, incapable of foreseeing the conclusion of a question and unable to see a matter through to its conclusion.

I tried to correct their distorted views by insisting that Lutheran pastors were also people of deep faith, firm moral standards, capable of doing responsible and great things in the church, nation, and state. I had only to point to our Slovak past and present history as clear evidences of that fact. The past was especially rich in examples of Lutheran contributions to the culture and morality of the Slovak nation.

More important for our situation were the differing reasons why the representatives of the two denominations were serving similar prison sentences. In most cases, the Roman Catholics were not imprisoned for religious reasons but rather for political opposition to the ruling regime. For many Catholic prisoners, it was a case of one totalitarian idea opposing another, one politically religious and the other politically secular. The majority of them were still resentful over the demise of the Slovak State, dominated and led chiefly by Catholic officials.

From a Christian viewpoint, one could not accept the expansionist politics of the Hlinka People's Party during the Slovak State era, when a totalitarian but Catholic Slovakia was being built according to Hitler's totalitarian German blueprint.

Every totalitarianism is not only intolerant but enslaving and destructive toward anything and anyone that differs from itself. Not one totalitarian system has anything in common with Christian universality. Jesus' Great Commission, "Go into all the world, and make disciples of all nations," has nothing in common with destructive totalitarianism with its policy of starving out its enemies and others who think or behave differently.

The invitation of Jesus, "Come to me, all who labor and are heavy-laden," is a constructive welcome of love into a community of love, peace, and rest to all who toil, suffer, hunger and yearn. Jesus' invitation is motivated by service and love for people. It offers the best resolution of mutual human relationships and optimal solutions of economic relationships—so that no one should suffer want.

Jesus' influence makes human values and potential blossom to the maximum degree, toward the very perfection of God, as God's aim is stated by Jesus: "Therefore be perfect, even as your Father in heaven is perfect." The presence of Jesus makes weak people strong, the fearful bold, the lowly great, the humble and simple wise and firm, the poor rich.

Jesus never preached or taught intolerance or enmity, despotism or cruelty. He condemned everything that has its origin in sin—

everything that serves sin and evil—and overcame and replaced them with service to God and sincere brotherly love. Totalitarian political systems do not and cannot do this, for they do not come from love but from force; and they do not lead to freedom but to enslavement, since they desire only to dominate and not to serve. In fact, because of their domination and control of power, they permit themselves to be called benefactors, because they consider domination and power to be the only good.

Over and against this greatness based on domination and power, Jesus sets greatness of service, of love, and of trust. How much of this did the so-called Christian Slovak State have and practice? Christianity, the church, and religion in general still suffer the bitter consequences of that politicized "Christianity."

This is how I debated and discussed the issue with them. Their reactions were interesting. The blindest and more firmly set in former positions of power reacted with anger, others with ridicule, and the insincere ones with haughtiness. But there were some, like Rudo Bašňák and Beňuška (who I believe was a deputy in the Hlinka People's Party), who reflected seriously and profoundly upon these problems and sought me out privately to further study and clarify these ideas.

My position had an even stronger effect on Janko Lang, a chaplain who came to me with the fervent admission: "Pastor, I admire you, and I envy you your stand and your present spiritual state of mind. You are here indeed for your religious convictions, for your mission work in the church and with youth. It was for that you were condemned. But I am deeply disturbed in my soul, because I—and not only I, but nearly all of those in prison here, priests, chaplains, monks, and professors—have been sentenced for espionage, theft of government property, for plotting murder and high treason, and other criminal offenses. In my investigation and trial I felt this most keenly. These offenses were used as fuel to denigrate and condemn religion, the church, the laity, and the clergy."

Then he explained how he came to be in prison. "The bishop in Trnava had taken several million crowns from the diocesan treasury and divided it among certain trustworthy priests. Together they organized a group escape to Austria and beyond. They had bought some weapons and procured boats to cross the Morava River.

"But the guides they hired turned out to be ŠTB agents! When they stepped into the boats, the guides turned them over to the ŠTB, who immediately arrested them, locked them up, took them to court, judged and condemned them.

"You can imagine how the atheistic communists gloated over that catch, with what delight they accused them of espionage, of anti-government activity, of the theft of government property, of being thieving priests and bishops, murderers and traitors!"

This young man of 30–35 years of age wept before me for the pain in his soul, for shame and humiliation. He would have been happy to suffer for Christ, for his faith, for his church, for mission work; but he was at the point of despair for having to suffer like a criminal for the listed and confessed crimes.

I comforted him by telling him that this was how the enemies of the church and of religion judge people who do not comprehend its God-intended meaning and mission, who exploit its mistakes and faults, but are themselves worse than what they are condemning. They have no remorse. They take what they did not earn by honest labor, they arrest and condemn innocent people, and they use every means to destroy the church and to exterminate religion. Their totalitarian system lives and acts by the principle that "the end justifies the means," a slogan they practice more consistently than anyone ever has. Such a system does not shun deceit, fraud, violence, or even murder. It has more weapons at hand than the pastors and priests they judge and condemn.

I led the young man in spirit to Jesus, who was also expelled from his nation, was handed over to pagans, mocked, tortured, and killed. This Jesus is able to judge our humiliation, hardships, and suffering. And this Jesus is the victor, the Lord of eternity, the Lord of life and death. He is the way, the truth, and the life.

The young man was ever so grateful to me for my sympathy and for the support he did not receive from his own church. But then neither did my own Lutheran church support me. The new leadership under Bishop Chabada distanced itself from me, would have nothing to do with me, and turned away the parishioners who interceded on my behalf—all because it was dangerous for the church and its leaders to touch my case. And what hurt the most was that even many of my fellow-pastors condemned me as well.

23
Serving out the Sentence

In general, life in prison was extremely rewarding for me. After the exhausting period of interrogation, I seemed to revive. I slept much and well, and enjoyed general good health. I refused to torture myself with needless worry. During the day I worked enthusiastically at whatever job I was given, whether in the mattress factory, in demolition work, or in the basket shop. I was able to maintain a cheerful attitude.

The long evenings were spent in discussions or exercising. We practiced simple calisthenics to stay in condition. During the first weeks in Leopoldov I developed my muscles to the point where I could do the "big bridge," the "small bridge," and the "snake man" easily. I could place both feet behind my head and walk on my hands like a frog. I could do exercises with a chair. And even in Ilava, I could do push-ups with one hand.

But by the third year of internment, I lost much of my strength and limberness. All of us noticed that effect of prison life on ourselves.

Apart from calisthenics, we played all kinds of games and held tournaments. It was wonderful to see the virtuosity we achieved as we made figurines out of bread, wood, and paper. Our games were not permitted but tolerated. When our guards were in a bad mood, they confiscated our creations.

Another pastime was reading. The prison library was comparatively extensive, but it had never been catalogued. It was managed by Dr. Tkáč, a lawyer from the vicinity of Bardejov. The poor man had been sentenced to 22 years for murder. Since I had officiated in Bardejov for more than two years, we got to know each other.

Tkáč had asked other prisoners to assist him in cataloging the library, but none of them were interested in the project. I volunteered to help. In just a couple of weeks, I had drawn up a catalog of authors and one of titles. The project proved to be of great benefit to me. I found out what books the library had, and I won the favor of Dr. Tkáč in lending me the books of my choice.

I was able to read a great deal, especially Soviet literature; but also the progressive literature of other countries: Polish, Hungarian, Bulgarian, Rumanian, Serbian, German, and others, besides various grammatical studies of the Slovak language. All in all, I gained a wide overview of socialistic literature. Few professors read as much on the subject as I was able to in confinement. I proved the proverb, "Whoever is not lazy will prosper." Not flinching from any task, I derived some benefit from every experience.

To this day, however, I sigh and regret that my church did not find my work desirable, and despite my repeated requests for reinstatement and restoration of my preaching license, it did not do so after my release from prison. Incomprehensible! How lamentable! Even though I never stopped working and living for the church as much as I could under all circumstances and conditions!

Despite my church body's denial of my request for restoration of my preaching license, I was able to perform pastoral services and do an effective mission ministry to a wider range of people than in civilian life. The fact that I was suffering the same conditions and treatment they were made my spiritual service to them so much more authentic and effective.

Just as the period of investigation is one of strict isolation, the serving of one's sentence is full of contacts with other people. During the period when there were 30 to 40 of us in a dormitory, I cite the following experience as typical of several where my pastoral background and training served to draw others into a contemplation of their spiritual needs and resources.

Daniel Vaculík and Jiří Chod were former officers of a district security (ONV) agency. Vaculík's father was a Baptist minister from Bratislava and was a high-ranking officer in the Baptist church administration. Vaculík himself was not especially active spiritually.

Chod was a Czech with no religious affiliation; he may even have been an atheist. The three of us worked side by side in the basket workshop. Chod was a skilled basket weaver. He and Vaculík were practicing their English when we got acquainted. Chod seemed to have no close friends and was quite forlorn. He liked listening to religious discussions and found the Lutheran theology more attractive than the Catholic.

Vaculík felt closer to the Lutheran views, though he said I did not fit the image of a Lutheran pastor. According to Vaculík, a pastor should be a quiet, loving, meek, humble, retiring person; whereas I was the professorial type, always searching, investigative, argumentative, cheerful, a lively debater, energetic, and one who looked at people from an intellectual point of view.

To Chod I lacked sanctimonious speech and a visible halo. Still, he did like my directness, earnestness, ebullience, endurance, and firmness of religious convictions.

It was interesting to receive such evaluations from different types of prisoners, to learn what kind of pastoral personality attracts or repels the seeker of religious truth.

When the two inmates were leaving for Jachymov, poor Chod begged me to give him 300 crowns from my account. He said he had no funds of his own, and that in Jachymov he would have access to a cafeteria, and that he would repay me if our paths ever crossed. I arranged for the transfer of funds with no expectation of having them repaid. Eventually I lost all track of them anyway. I did, however, get a souvenir from Chod: a border for a basket I had woven when we worked together, and which I still have to this day.

Worth mentioning also were my ties with inmates who were engineers and project designers. There were a number of genuine persons among them, but just as many weaklings, whimpering cowards, and even weaker characters. They ran the gamut of character traits from the highly intellectual, moral, and religious people to the tyrants, cursers, murderers, boors, thieves, and brutes. Most of the political prisoners were of the former type.

As every beauty stands out more prominently in prison, so every ugliness is exaggerated. In the prisoner's hopeless situation, every injustice is more painful. In order to surmount these realities, one needs more than intellect; one must have moral and spiritual convictions. Only so can one explain why prisoners in identical circumstances came to me to counsel them in their difficulties and problems, or simply to be calmed and comforted.

I also found some strong individuals among the many I met, young as well as old. They didn't have to be highly educated. They were often ordinary people who were nevertheless profound, serious, morally- and spiritually-grounded, genuine persons.

123

24

The Constant Dream of Freedom

The yearning for freedom never leaves a prisoner. And we nourished it by feeding the feeling of innocence, the conviction of truth, and the denial of wrongdoing. We did not entertain any expiatory expectation of our end. Freedom was bonded in us with truth and justice, integrity and faithfulness, with self-esteem and honesty. Insofar as we possessed these qualities and traits, we created an inner freedom for ourselves even within prison walls and bars.

Every escape attempt kindled in us a longing for freedom. And there were many of them.

To mention one instance: 40 to 50 prisoners worked in the tailor shop. Two of them—one former sergeant (a young professional soldier, a Czech by birth, whose name I don't recall) and a friend of his—arranged with the supervisor that the two of them would sweep the shop regularly every morning before working hours while the others were taking their daily exercise walk.

The two inmates learned that the sacristy of the Ilava Catholic chapel was directly beneath their sewing machine. They plotted to break through the arch below their floor and lower themselves into the sacristy while the priest was doing the mass.

Every morning, during their sweeping period, they would burrow a hole through the floor. Over several weeks they carried out the debris with their sweepings into the trash containers in the prison yard. When they figured they were close to breaking through the ceiling below, they decided to make their escape.

They waited for the mass to begin. Cutting the final portion of the hole, however, took longer than they had anticipated. Just as they were lowering themselves into the sacristy, the mass ended.

The escapees were too late to mingle with the prisoners attending the mass. When the priest returned, he noticed a figure in a worker's apron and sounded the alarm, informing the warden of the escape attempt.

The ŠTBs came, hauled them out of the chapel, and placed them in the correctional ward. There they were interrogated, beaten, tortured, and sentenced to additional time.

The whole event upset us greatly. Looking at the matter purely through prisoners' eyes, we blamed the priest who foiled their escape, and we regretted that the longing for freedom was thwarted once again. The hope never died, however, despite failure and disillusionment, despite formidable obstacles, despite brutal suppression.

I recall Lieutenant Čukan, under a sentence of 20 years, who made more than three escape attempts, was always caught, yet continued to plan another escape. He lived only for that purpose.

I found a spiritual application of this yearning for freedom in the experience of the person who is awakened by the Lord's call and perseveres in his determination to escape from sin and death into the freedom of God's children. That escape is possible as "everything is possible to the one who believes," but only to the one who believes in Jesus Christ, the God-sent liberator of captive humanity.

I myself had only two opportunities to escape prison. The first was in December, when we went to the Union of Agricultural Workers (JRD) to dig potatoes from under the snow. The second time I persuaded our warden to choose me to help cut apart a kitchen range and remove it from a wall, leaving an opening we were then to fill. He agreed to have me work on the project, and I got a glimpse of the world outside the prison walls.

25

Never-Ending Hunger

With rations meager as they were, the prisoners were always hungry. Even in prison, society was graded, and food was rationed according to work: very hard, hard, light, and none. When there was no work, everyone hungered.

Once, during such a crisis, Professor Arany surprised me. Somewhere in the trash he found a whole loaf of bread, hard and covered with green mold. All excited, he brought it to us. Astounded, I asked him if he really intended us to eat it.

"Why, of course!" he replied very self-evidently.

He then placed the loaf on a stove, baked it through and through, from bottom to top, and we all ate it and enjoyed it. We thought of the mold as penicillin. Fortunately, we didn't get sick from it.

There were times when we dined better. With money in the allowance account, one could buy some bread and margarine, or scare up an onion, cocoa, and some tea to round out the prison fare.

As repulsive as I found it to look at informers, still, when I saw wretched Danek—who was often taken away by the ŠTB for a day or two at a time—pitifully watching us eat, I cut off a big slice of bread, smeared it with margarine, covered it with onion slices, and handed it to him. Many of the priests criticized me for lowering myself to help a robber and informer. He was indeed a robber, and maybe an informer too; but he was hungry, and I never regretted sharing bread with him. The hungry should be fed and the sick healed.

I was on the receiving end, too, when I was very hungry. And I will never forget how happy I was when someone shared a ration with me. I have already mentioned some such benefactors, but I want to recall a certain Mr. Horný. A German by birth, he was married to a Slovak woman and lived near Lučenec. He had been imprisoned for embezzling and speculating with ration cards for workers on a construction job where he was either the boss or foreman. When our paths crossed, he was already over 60.

Though a Roman Catholic, he came to me, no doubt because we came from the same region. In prison he was working on a construction gang and used to get an additional ration of food. Often he would offer me a share of his extra portion. I accepted the treat from him, not only because at his age he didn't need as much to eat, but chiefly because he looked to me for some kind of moral support.

Horný had lost a son about my age in the War. The Catholic priests faulted me for accepting a piece of bread from someone so morally low and dirty. But I saw a human being in him, and he appreciated it.

The poor man died in Ilava of a heart attack. When I left prison, his widow sought me out, asking for details about his life and death in prison, information I was glad to provide.

The second case of a death in the Ilava camp was that of a certain Bokor from Lučenec. He had been sentenced for Hungarian irre-dentist activity, like the aforementioned professor Arany. Bokor had suffered a nervous breakdown in prison. Mentally ill, he did all kinds of irrational things. At first he was placed in a correctional ward and then in a solitary cell, where he died. The cause of his death was not reported, but it was rumored that he was in such a state that he ate his own excrement.

Others suffered greater or lesser distress. Once I went with Paška, the sergeant of the guard, to get something from the store-house. I accompanied him to the solitary confinement wing, where he had some work to do. We arrived at the ground floor just as meals were being distributed. As a somewhat veteran prisoner, I tried to see if I recognized any of the men in solitary.

There was "Daňo" [Daniel] Vesely! I whispered to him, "Daňo, is that you?"

He lifted his head, smiled weakly, and said, "It's me."

Paška stopped me at once from conversing with Vesely any more. It was strange and sad to see him in jail, too. He knew of my im-prisonment, but I knew nothing about his until then.

I knew Vesely from the *Gymnázium* in Martin. According to a certain Jakubčík, he had visited me at the parsonage in Háj on some mission. When they locked me up, he was already at the seminary in Bratislava, where a group of students at the school of theology formed a popular group of like-minded seminarians. Some incident involving the group of Confessionalists, which included Vesely and Oravec, got them arrested and imprisoned.

And then I come across Daňo in solitary! And how did Straško become his cellmate? I don't even know how Straško got placed in solitary, since I left him in the mattress shop.

Daňo allegedly suffered severe physical abuse from the guards in solitary. I didn't meet him until the first days of May 1953 when we were being selected for release during the amnesty that was announced when President Gottwald died and was replaced by Zapotocký.

26

Prospects of Amnesty

I believe I have sufficiently described the situation in prison during my stay. Essentially, these events were multiplied in numerous variations. I don't know if we were becoming dulled somehow, but the experiences of others were not as interesting to us. In the course of time, we learned who our informers were; and when new ones took their place, we were no longer afraid of them.

The days settled into a gray routine. There was little excitement. The usual debates never got off the ground. A kind of torpidity settled over us. Even in our jobs nothing unusual happened.

Into this dullness came the news of Stalin's death. Suddenly the prison came alive. There was much talk about the Stalin era and speculation as to what would happen in the Soviet Union after his death.

We had hardly finished discussing the aftermath of Stalin's death when, a few days after Stalin's funeral in March 1953, Klement Gottwald, the president of Czechoslovakia, died. This event caused a rush of excitement among us.

Gottwald had scarcely been buried when the veteran prisoners began talking about an amnesty when the new president would take office. Of course, no one knew how widespread such an amnesty would be and whom it would include. Still, everyone was sure that the political course of events would not change either in our country or in the USSR, although we know today that they did change significantly in both places.

If the prospects for release by amnesty were vague at this time, any efforts on my behalf by the Lutheran church officials were equally uncertain. I had the unqualified support of my family, who visited me regularly during prescribed times, and received letters from home only in response to my own correspondence. But at Christmas, Easter, and on my birthday, I received dozens of greetings, which, surprisingly, were delivered to me. From the hundreds of pastors, I received a greeting only from Ján Horváth from Blatnice, and, at the beginning of my incarceration, from Pastor Šolc, my predecessor in Háj, who represented me from the start and was silenced only by his death.

The church leaders under Bishop Chabada showed no interest in me, even though they were in constant contact with my family and knew the contents of my letters to them. I suspect that Bishop Čobrda's silence in my case was due to suppression of his interest and intercessions on my behalf by higher-ups and his successors.

Darina Banciková, in her *Memoirs* (*Spomienky*), states that at the beginning of 1951—it must have been after March 14, 1951, the day of my imprisonment—she went to Bishop Čobrda's home to type some kind of memorandum which the bishop wanted to present to the representative of Minister Fierlinger upon his visit to the general bishop's office in Liptovský Mikuláš.

She writes, "The memorandum was concerned about the protection of the diaconate, of the amnesty of Pastor Uhorskai, and of all pastors who had been deprived of their certification. There were then just a couple of these whose licenses had been taken away more for teaching religion than for any other reason."

Minister Fierlinger's representative, Dr. Eckard, actually came to Liptovský Mikuláš and received the memorandum together with the resignation of Bishop General Čobrda as well as that of Superintendent DE Peter Zatko. But no one knows anything about the amnesty. It seems someone had deceived Bishop Čobrda. Could it have been someone in the church administration?

The leadership of the SECAV under Bishop Chabada tried to stamp out my footprints after me, but they revealed no effort to take a stand in my case, no effort to become familiar with the case of one of their brothers, no effort to defend the church's pastor and to help him. I believe this negligence was due to fear and helplessness in the main, but in some cases, one might ascribe it to careerism.

I will not go into the matter any further, since I did not expect any help at all from the church leaders. I did not see then—nor for a long time thereafter—the [true] church in the leadership of the church. I find the church present only where Christ himself is present. And he was with me before my trial, during my trial, in prison, and after my release from prison. He was faithful to me then, and he is faithful to me now. I pray that I may be as faithful to him.

There was more understanding of my situation and of my suffering among individual pastors—even though some may have thought I was overly rash and frank and that I unduly complicated my situation. I think I have convinced those who are following this account of mine that I have no desire for cheap martyrdom nor of any dubious glory, but only for our Lord's church and for the Lord himself.

I know I am far from perfect. I also know that today I would do things with greater deliberation, especially since I have gone through an exceptional life-school and have acquired experiences I never had before. Nevertheless, I stand by my behavior during that period and assume complete responsibility for it. I am not ashamed of my actions. In fact, in a certain sense, I am proud of them.

27

Free at Last?

I return to the final days of my imprisonment. If I said earlier that we all longed for freedom, then with the preparation of the amnesty, freedom was almost within reach of some of us, and we all longed for it even more fervently. That was true even of those who had minimal prospects for amnesty. The thought of freedom preoccupied us even when we didn't talk about it. It burned and glowed in us; it was the subject of our prayers.

By the middle of April 1953, we received more definite reports of the scope of the amnesty. Many inmates applied the reports to their own case and became more optimistic. It was difficult to find a correct perspective in such an intense situation. Especially since none of us had read the announcement of the amnesty, nor did we have access to an expanded newspaper report.

I don't recall the date when the new president, Zapotocký, issued the decree. It was probably May 1, 1953. Nor do I remember the day we learned of it in prison, nor do I intend to search it out. That's not important. What is important is that it arrived and that it brought joy and hope to many prisoners.

How was I awaiting the amnesty? I was convinced that it would include me, and that I would be among the first to go free in a short time. Was that being overly optimistic, realistic, unrealistic? I didn't really care. The reality for me was my comparatively short sentence of three years, of which I had already completed two years and two months. The other qualifying factor in the equation was the charge against me: that the misuse of my religious activity in the anti-Marxist training of young people was not expressly an anti-government offense.

I was truly sure I was going home. And yet I had no feeling of gratitude toward the president of the republic for proclaiming an amnesty. I harbored a lively feeling of innocence as well as a feeling that injustice and wrong had been done me, which the amnesty did not remove but merely shortened. Nor was I the only one who had such feelings and convictions. Everyone did. Indeed, I never for a moment regretted what I had done to get arrested, because I had never considered my activity to be criminal. I was aware only of the injustice I was suffering, and I thanked God that it was coming to an end.

It was in this kind of mood that the last days transpired—and badly at that. We were certain that the amnesty had been decreed and that it applied to us also. We would have been happiest if we were going home immediately. Our work slumped as the warden tried to settle us down by telling us the process would take some time until the procurator examined all the verdicts and determined whether the amnesty applied to a certain prisoner or not, or to what extent, and when the prisoner would be set free, at once or in several months.

Although we felt bad about the delay, none of us did anything foolish. We went to work every morning as usual, but our production fell far below normal. Warden Baťalik understood the situation. After supper he permitted us to gather in small groups to discuss how the amnesty would affect our respective cases.

I shared with my friends my conviction that I would soon be going home to freedom. Eng. Kramár and Eng. Klein came to me from the engine room, where many of my friends and acquaintances worked, and asked me to deliver some letters for them, which I promised gladly to do—and did. We had been prisoners long enough to know how to get letters sent to me and have me then direct them to the right address.

Finally a definite sign appeared. One morning we did not go to work. In the wards, the tension had reached its climax. The ŠTBs walked up and down the corridors calling out the prisoners, who gathered their knapsacks and followed them out of their cells. Where to? No one knew, not those who were leaving nor those who were staying behind. But the ones leaving were understandably more excited than those who were left behind. The latter were devastated by the news.

I remember one such unfortunate prisoner who suffered that bitter disappointment. He was a Jesuit named Mittach, serving an 8- to 10-year sentence. I saw him press against the gate when the others were leaving and ask an ŠTB agent if he was going to be leaving too. The ŠTB was so busy that he could only glance at the list and tell the man that he was not on it. Poor Mittach was left shattered and sobbing—a 40-year-old man in the prime of life.

Although I pitied him in his situation, I had no doubts that I would be set free. I noticed that the names were being called alphabetically. Since *U* is quite far from the beginning, I was obviously impatient. Finally my name was called. I shook hands with all the prisoners who were not leaving then, said a few words of farewell, and headed for freedom.

I thought I would be going directly to the storehouse to pick up my things and go straight home. But hardly! I was led into a large room where several dozen people were gathered. Their eyes glowed with joy. Many of those whom I knew greeted me and rejoiced with me. It was there that I found Martin Straško and, moments later, Daňo Vesely.

We sat on our knapsacks and waited. Waiting—that inevitable element of prison life—lasted a long time. At least longer than we expected. We spent the night in that large room without beds.

All night long the three of us conversed. Only then were we joined by Noška, another Lutheran pastor. I don't know why he was sentenced, though it may have been for some criminal offense. Later a Calvinist preacher from the eastern part of Slovakia joined us. He shared with us information we had not heard before: how the officials behaved toward pastors and their wives in the Low Carpatho-Russian region where he was a pastor. For example, how the wives of arrested pastors, when their salary was discontinued, resorted to selling their clothes and household goods in order to survive and feed their children until they found some employment. Since this pastor was imprisoned he had lost track of his family and didn't know in what condition he would find them. He needed our sympathy and encouragement.

Only the next morning did we finally board the green transports that would take us to freedom. Straško, Daňo, and I theologized a great deal, as though we were still in prison and not heading from captivity to freedom. Martin merely smiled at Daňo and me as we went on debating even on the road.

We guessed we were being taken to Bratislava. And that is where we were unloaded, at the military prison at No. 74 Krížna Street. This time we were treated more leniently than at our first detention or in Leopoldov. During our medical examination I met Dr. Stodola, the physician and writer, who was also enjoying his freedom. It was good talking to him and to receive valuable information from him. I introduced myself to him as a Lutheran pastor and Daňo as a Lutheran seminarian.

In his book *Sad Times, Sad Home* Stodola mentions us on page 156: "Among them were a Lutheran pastor and a seminarian from Trenčín." I was that pastor, and Daňo Vesely was the seminarian. The reference to Trenčín was inaccurate. The other Lutheran clergy, whom I mention in my account and who were also with me, did not introduce themselves to Stodola, which is why he does not refer to them but includes them among the Catholic clergy.

In Bratislava Daňo and I tried to get lodging in the same room. Compared to our prison cells, the accommodations were like a hotel: the rooms had two beds and were incomparably more civilized than Ilava, Leopoldov, or the detention center in Bratislava. Straško was so considerate that he arranged for us to room together, even though it was only for two nights and two days, May 6-8, 1953. Still it was a special treat for us, since we were able to exchange opinions on various matters and events.

Daňo was not at all despondent over his internment. Though thin, his spirits were fresh and lively. We philosophized and theologized as enthusiastically as fellow-students. We also sang some hymns, including one I mentioned earlier, "Hell Rages in Vain," sung to *Es Ist das Heil.* To Daňo it sounded like a militant anthem.

In the privacy of our room, Daňo had an opportunity to give me his version of the reason for his imprisonment. He had had the same experiences I had with the officialdom of the church. They distanced themselves from him just as they had from me. Their allegations against him and Oravec (whom I had not met) before the court were extremely unfavorable as well as untrue. The student "biologists," as they were called, were openly hostile, so much so that I could not comprehend why they were enrolled in the seminary, where they turned theological debates into ŠTB denunciations.

It would be better for Vesely to prepare a full first-hand account of his experience to supplement this sketchy report.

On the morning of May 8, a Friday, some 60 to 80 of us were brought together into a larger room. Procurator Dr. P. Winter, the same one who prosecuted me at my trial, launched into a half-hour lecture, in which he told us how grateful we ought to be to the state for freeing us before our sentences were completed. He made a point of stressing how he remembered what stubborn enemies we were of the people's democratic system, and that the government's aim was to rehabilitate us.

The time we spent in prison, he went on, was just a part of our re-education. Now we were going to be re-educated through the process of regular daily work. It was up to us how long this process would take. If we could present evidence of our satisfactory reha-bilitation, we would be eligible for reinstallation into pastoral service.

His speech was so provocative that it was all we could do not to explode. However, we suppressed our indignation rather than risk losing or delaying our entry into freedom.

Our possessions, which had been stored for us, were now re-turned. In my case, significantly, they did not return a penny of the funds they had confiscated when they arrested me, saying that, ac-cording to the verdict, the funds became the property of the state.

This fact was confirmed for me by an ŠTB named Varga, who checked the records as a personal favor, because we both came from Lučenec. At the same time he advised me as to how I could withdraw my money by referring to my verdict. Since I was never given a copy of my verdict nor any voucher from the court, he searched out the number of my verdict and sentence: 3 TS III, 58/51–53. I copied it and have kept it until now.

Finally, we received our release papers from the headquarters of the regional prison in Bratislava. Mine had the number 883 z.k/1953, and states that "Pavel Uhorskai, born March 2, 1919, in To-mašovce, in the Lučenec district, was by the amnesty of the president of the Republic released from captivity this day, May 4, 1953." The document bore the official oblong seal of the Bratislava correctional institution and an illegible signature.

This was the one and only document related to my trial and imprisonment that I ever received. Otherwise I had only heard the charges, and the verdict was never given to me.

28

Free—But Not Completely

We were then loaded into buses with drawn shades and transported into the city proper. We were sad that Daňo did not go with us. Even with the amnesty, he still had some three months to serve. Nevertheless, we parted as close comrades, not at all depressed but with a happy outlook toward the future as becomes believers.

Two buses were taking us somewhere in the direction of the National Gallery. There the ŠTBs led us into a building that looked like a tenement. Somewhere on the first floor, we were led into two or three apartments and ordered to wait for private interviews.

For the first time we got a good look at each other, and the sight was a strange one. Until then we had seen one another only in prison uniforms. Some of us still had decent clothes, but I must have looked rather miserable in the clothes I was wearing when I was arrested, patched here and there, and in which I had rolled around for eight months without cleaning or pressing. They were in fact no better than the prison garb I had been wearing. Martin Straško had on a pair of borrowed coveralls, because he had sent all his clothes home.

It was a long wait before the monotony was broken. Prisoners began coming out of the interviews, merely throwing up their hands to express their uncertainty as to what was going on. Before long, someone more familiar with the procedures told us what was happening.

My turn came almost two hours later. I entered a room where three men and a woman were sitting. The leader was J. Kmeť; one of the other men was Fajnor; and the third seemed to be an ŠTB agent. I don't recall the woman's name.

Kmeť opened the interview with a sneer. "Well, you really did a fine job in Háj."

I said, "I think I did very little in Háj; I was there such a short time. You should have left me there longer; I would have done more."

"Is that so? Why, Háj is still in shambles!"

I decided not to argue further. After lecturing me about how bad and ungrateful I was, he advised me to be thankful that I was getting out of prison. And that gratitude to the state I was to express where the state needed it most—in the mines.

At that point I said I was under the impression that I had been released with a "C" classification, hence unfit for work in the mines. Kmet' told me not to worry, that medical care was available for mine workers.

His remarks ended with a recommendation that I go to the mines as a member of a volunteer brigade. I protested again that my state of health would not allow me to do any kind of mine labor, and I requested to be placed on some government property or in some industry near my residence.

At this, Fajnor paused magnanimously and said that one year of voluntary brigade work would suffice. The nearest factories with organized recruits were the Slovak chemical works in Likier. I was to report there.

I nodded, and the interview was over.

Not everyone received the same kind of assignment. Some did not have to report at all for voluntary brigade duty. Evidently, the jobs were determined by some kind of code. I soon discovered that the old grading system in effect before my imprisonment still applied.

29

Heading for Home at Last

We were then indeed set free. Martin Straško, Noška, and the Calvinist pastor wanted badly to go to Blaho's, to eat some more decent food than they had had in prison. So we went. But I was restless and impatient—I was anxious to head for home.

Instead of going to the train station, we went to Konventná Street. On the way we met Dr. Oberuč, who recognized me immediately, took me by the arm, and walked me around Trinity Church to Koza Street and on to Konventná Street. While he inquired about my experiences, he himself spoke very vaguely and generally about conditions on the outside, at the seminary, and in the church. It was nevertheless evident from his remarks that he did not agree with the current administration. The conversation was soon over, and we parted.

I then went with Straško to the seminary. Even though it was mid-afternoon, we did not catch any of the faculty members there. In the student dormitory, I found some theological students, introduced myself, but found no one I knew among them.

All the time I was carrying a souvenir from prison: an inlaid box that "Jožko" [Jozef] Nadeniček had made for me long ago. I didn't care to carry it any longer, so I gave it to student Surkoš, who was glad to receive it.

From there we went to Dr. Cibulka's parsonage [see Appendix C]. We found him interested in us, in our experiences and opinions. He had no inkling at the time that in less than a year he would have to leave Bratislava for Háj, my former station. When he offered to treat us with something, I asked for a glass of milk, which I had not drunk in nearly three years. He gladly granted my request, and I thanked him profusely.

After about 15 minutes, we left for the train station. Under my arm I carried my only possessions: a large Bible Bishop Ruppeldt had sent me while I was still in the detention center in Žilina, and the booklet *Words of Comfort.*

Since I had a letter for Eng. E. Kramár and Eng. Klein's family in Vrútky [a suburb of Martin], I took the express train to Žilina, arriving there shortly after midnight. Late as it was, I interrupted my trip to stop at the parsonage there. I awoke Br. [Brother] Milan Dudáš, apologized for the nighttime disturbance, and handed him the letter to relay to the family. I was there hardly more than a minute. I promised Milan I would visit him and talk to him at a later date, and left for home on the next train.

In Turčianské Teplice, I sent greetings via the station shoemaker to my friends in Háj, telling them that I was coming home from prison. It was still night.

In Zvolen I met my first fellow-countryman, Janko Korin, who, seeing me from a distance, ran toward me and greeted me heartily.

I finally arrived at home Saturday, May 9, 1953, around eight o'clock in the morning. It was the beginning of a spring day, and people were already working in the fields. The aroma of spring filled the village.

My friends welcomed me with joy and tears. I had to tell them everything. The words must have tumbled out of my mouth incoherently. How could it have been otherwise, considering the excitement and the multitude of experiences to review? But the stress of the previous two weeks was adding to my fatigue. More than anything, I wanted to sleep.

Other visitors came, but as soon as they left, I fell into a deep sleep.

Sunday morning, exactly at eight o'clock, my friends from Háj arrived to visit me. Our meeting was highly emotional. They inquired about my health, my experiences, everything. I assured them that, thank God, I was feeling fine. They were pleased with my outward appearance and with my positive attitude. Then they filled me in on the news of the Háj parish, about my successor, and how they had been waiting for my return.

I had to inform them that I still had a year of volunteer brigade duty to perform. After that I would request an amnesty from the balance of my sentence (the loss of civil rights for five years), because the loss of my civil rights prevented me from obtaining government approval for my preaching license.

They were neither satisfied nor cheered by that news. But since nothing could be done about it, I asked them to greet the congregation for me, and I thanked them for their concern for me and my situation. I promised to visit them as soon as I had rested. They said goodbye and departed on the evening train.

It felt good to be home again. Even though I was poor as a church mouse, the love of my friends was worth more to me than all the riches in the world. I didn't worry about "what I would eat and drink, or what I would wear." I was free!! And everything pleased me. Not even the untimely snowfall—unusual for the tenth of May—dampened my joy.

In church a new surprise awaited me: Pastor Chochol was gone. He had been replaced by an administrator from the general bishop's office: Dr. L. Lanštiak, who was coolly received by the parishioners, and whom I remembered from my trial in the state court in Bratislava, where he wept throughout the entire proceedings.

A few days later I set out to make some visits. I called on Bishop Ruppeldt in Žilina. I returned the Bible and *Words of Comfort,* and thanked him for his solicitude, which meant so much to me in prison. I asked him to express my appreciation to the sisters who managed to deliver those precious gifts to me in prison and for the favor of washing my linens for me.

After that I went to Liptovský Mikuláš and made a call on Bishop General Dr. Vladimir Čobrda. We discussed the situation in the church and the difficulties it was facing under communist oppression. He complained of the secret struggles and intrigues against him by some of the church leaders. I urged him not to give in or retreat but to fight, because the church needed him. I would like to think that I encouraged him with my ardor and optimism.

He was happy to see me out of prison, but he had no idea when I would be able to resume my pastoral service. He seemed to be very, very powerless, and was unable to lift my spirits, though that was not necessary. Instead, I encouraged him, urging him to endure the battle for the church, for it was becoming a battle against potential enemies of the Christian church itself.

Čobrda did not, however, see them as such; but he said he admired my conviction and courage. When I repeated in the strongest terms that he must not retreat or surrender, since he was after all the bishop of the church and the Lord of the church would hold

141

him responsible for his leadership and faithfulness, he sadly placed both hands on my shoulders and said, "Dear brother, if only I were 30 years old!"

Tears filled his eyes, for he was more than 70 then. I pitied him as a person, but I could not excuse him from his responsibility for the church. Evidently he did not resent me for my pleadings, as Darina Banciková reports in her memoirs.

It must have been on this trip, too, that I met Brother Jozef Juráš. He had just returned from his first detention—an investigation that lasted several months. He looked quite bad. His face was swollen and pale, and he had a shaggy beard, for he was unable to shave because of facial eczema. However, his eyes shone with enthusiasm.

Juráš complained of the harsh treatment he received during his interrogation. He was under suspicion chiefly for his visit to the U.S. and for his ties with Dr. Igor Bella. For those reasons he was accused of espionage for a foreign power and treason. In the brief time we had together, he could not go into detail.

Juráš's detention was just the beginning of his prison experience. Later he was jailed again and given a severe sentence. I am not qualified to give a full accounting of his case, since I know so little about it, even though I participated in one of his rehabilitation hearings in Košice at the end of summer, 1959. My impression was that imprisonment was more than he could bear. [The reader may refer to J. Vajda's article on Jozef Juráš in *The Lutheran Witness* (October 31, 1976), "But the Heavenly Choir Sang."]

I must affirm here that neither in my court investigation nor in Juráš's were we accused of complicity in our offenses. His hearing was based on entirely different grounds, for he was seen as a potential candidate for the office of bishop of the SECAV and was suspected of preparing an opposition leadership role in the church. Someone could fill this gap in our church's history by organizing all the events of this martyr's life from documents in the possession of his family and associates.

30

Life in the "Volunteer Brigades"

In the beginning of June 1953, I joined the ranks of the "volunteer brigades" as a woodchopper in the Slovak chemical works in Likier. It was a hard job unloading logs from trucks, then splitting them into pieces 4″ in diameter and placing them into frames to be picked up by the bosses from the plant. We were outdoors in all kinds of weather. Although the work was hard, it had its advantages. In the fresh air, my hands and arm muscles were strengthened remarkably. Before long, I could match the best brigade workers as well as the full-time laborers.

When I was consigned to the plant, I had to undergo a physical examination, during which Dr. Kaprinay discovered (on the X-ray) a spot the size of a 10-halier coin [the size of a dime] on the right side of my lungs. He recommended I have it checked. But it didn't seem to be anything serious. I think he merely wanted to spare me the heavy labor, which I didn't mind. My troubles were of a different nature. I will relate one case.

Every morning there was a 10-minute interval at the beginning of the work period. It was meant to be a briefing for the job of the day, during which the special details of the assignment were explained, together with some indoctrination of the political implications of the work.

The bosses responsible for the briefings made light of them and had us merely read some articles from *Pravda*, *Práca*, or some other periodical. More than once the boss asked me to conduct the 10-minute period.

One such time occurred that summer. At the time a Communist rally was going on in Prague (I think it was the tenth such gathering). The papers were filled with minute details of the event, including a report by then President Viliam Široký in which he said something

143

about agriculture. He stated that, despite the program of collectivization, agriculture continued to have problems due to a lack of professional staff.

When I read the report, I explained exactly what "lack of professional staff" meant. I said the Union of Agricultural Workers (JRD) was composed chiefly of small farmers, former servants, farmhands, and people with no professional training, many of whom lacked the most basic practical experience. This, I pointed out, was causing problems in the JRD. Running a JRD project covering 2,500 to 4,000 acres was not the same as farming five to eight acres or working as a farmhand or drafted laborer.

The workers understood what I was saying and were satisfied with my explanation. So was the boss, as we went to our task. The next "Ten Minutes" followed a similar pattern—and our work went on as usual.

About a week later I was called into the boss's office around 9 A.M. A ZNB agent, Balúch by name, was there. He began accusing me of agitating workers against the JRD, that I was belittling and insulting the officers of the union, and so on.

I defended myself, saying I had said no such thing, nor had I even had any such idea. When I appealed to Hoško, the boss, to tell the man what I had said in the briefings, he remained silent as a fish.

I then invited the agent to come to the briefing period the next morning and ask those who heard me what I had said. Balúch brushed my invitation aside, telling me I had no right to advise him what he should do.

He finished the hearing, made some notes, but didn't give me anything to sign.

When I returned to my job some two hours later, I told the men that I had been investigated. They shook their heads and said the accusations were not true, but that someone had it in for me for some reason and had reported me.

The next morning during the briefing, I told how I had been investigated the day before. Those present repeated that the charges were trumped up, that someone was out to get me. I asked if two or three of them would witness on my behalf that the charges were false, that I had said nothing of the sort. At first they promised to do so; but when the time came, they lost their nerve.

144

Another two weeks went by, but Balúch didn't show up again. I learned from Jakubčík, a fellow-worker in the next section, whose wife worked in the district procurator's office in Hnúšťa, that a notice of my "criminal" activity was already in the hands of the procurator of the ZNB.

Hearing this, I pleaded with the boss and workers more urgently to go with me to the procurator and to witness to the actual truth. But no one was willing to do so!

When four or five more days had elapsed, I made my appeal again during the briefing period for at least two men to accompany me to the procurator. But again, no one wanted to go. I was really in a bind.

The problem was compounded by the fact that the procurator absolutely refused to grant me a hearing. I tried all kinds of approaches, but nothing came of them. The procurator sent word that he was unable to receive me. What was I to do to clear myself?

Once again I explained to my co-workers that I was not guilty of the allegations. They agreed I was not guilty, but they were afraid to go to the procurator. Those were the days of widespread intimidation.

Finally, two workers from the next section, Vojtech Sendrei from Hnúšťa and Karol Sendrei from Kokava—both gypsies—came and said that since the others were afraid, they would go with me to the procurator and testify to the actual situation.

The procurator continued to refuse to see me. Actually he was afraid! Not of me, but of the government. Finally, thanks to Jakubčík's wife, an elementary school teacher, and Mr. Palečka, the procurator agreed to see me—but only after office hours, around 6 P.M.

Procurator Javor was alone in his office. He gave me Balúch's report to read. The introduction stated his justification for the charge.

"The subject herein named is unable, as a former pastor, to forget the old golden days, and now, as a determined enemy of the people's democratic system, agitated against the collectives, saying they did not know how to work, that they consisted only of shepherds, farmhands, and hired hands ... "

I explained to the procurator what had actually taken place, and I said there were witnesses who could verify my remarks. He replied that witnesses were unnecessary, that he would not present the complaint to the court, but would give me a declaration to sign; and that if I were to commit a similar transgression in the future, he would use this accusation against me.

I signed it willingly.

Then he began talking to me confidentially. In a completely friendly manner, he asked me about my court case. Now and then he mentioned something that surprised me. For example, when I said that all my books, sermons, literary works, histories, and other writings were confiscated and never returned, he told me I would never get them back, because they were all definitely burned. [See Appendix D.]

I was touched as well as upset by this news. But it was true, as I was notified by Procurator Urban when I was being rehabilitated in 1969.

And so, another unpleasant event—but typical of that era—had ended.

When I related to the men back at the labor camp what had happened, they said they had found out who had reported me: a certain Capcík. I merely listened without drawing any conclusions about the man. I knew he had not done this on his own initiative. He was merely the instrument of others who had orders from above to watch me and to use every opportunity to bring me to trial again and to isolate me from society.

That was how people's characters were deformed. Decent people became snitches; guardians of justice became distorters and destroyers of the truth; friends and brothers became unfeeling and unheeding fellow-travelers on the road of life. Please, God, grant love!

In the same summer of 1953, I began to experience a similar attitude at home also. During the threshing of grain a fire broke out from stalks piled next to a threshing machine. According to unprejudiced reports, the stalks caught fire from the uncovered exhaust pipe of a tractor that was hauling away the threshed grain.

Nevertheless there were members of the Public Security and employees of the District Committee of the Slovak Communist Party who claimed that I—the "Reverend Pastor"—was the arsonist!

What had actually happened?

That particular afternoon, a companion and I were going by wagon to the forest in Sedemchotáre for a load of wood. We passed by the threshing crew on a road some 30 to 50 meters from them. When we had gone about a kilometer farther, we noticed the stalks of grain beginning to burn. We stopped at once, turned the wagon around and hurried to help put out the fire.

In the ten minutes it took to get to the burning stalks, it was already too late to save them. I kept on putting out the fire until the flames died. In fact, I joined the night watch at the site of the fire just in case it started burning again.

Only one of my fellow-townsmen defended me against the slander during the investigation. He had been detained and questioned in connection with the fire, because he was there as one of the threshers. When he was repeatedly asked whether I was the one who set the fire when I was passing by, he firmly denied even the possibility of my doing so. No matter how much pressure they exerted on him, he would not change his testimony.

This was a tactic that was used against the church and its pastors. They were accused of the most incredible acts and then vilified, condemned, and punished.

Although the situation around me in Likier calmed down, I made an effort to get home and find work that would allow me to stay there continually. With the help of acquaintances and fellow-students, including some who belonged to the Slovak Communist Party, I succeeded in getting the approval of the District National Committee to work off the remainder of my "volunteer brigade" sentence in the Underground Construction Company in Banská Bystrica, as a construction worker under the Lučenec construction administration.

So it was that from February 2, 1954, I lived at home and went to work in Lovinobaňa, where a school and dormitory were being built. There I worked as a warehouseman.

On that job I had peace. Not only that, but when my fellow-workers learned that I was a pastor, they treated me with respect and addressed me as "Reverend Sir"—which, of course, soon elicited a protest from party members.

I performed my warehouse duties conscientiously, even beyond the minimum demands, and found that I was adept at handling projects, invoices, and the construction agenda in general. Eventually, my superior entrusted me with making purchase invoices, following budget and production estimates, recording material supplies, and preparing production orders.

After three years and four months, the company administration appointed me manager of its Technical Material Supply department. I did not care to accept the appointment; handling supplies is a highly complicated operation and something is always missing in the system. Because everyone is dependent on "the system," everyone tends to nag the supply master—especially if that person is a pastor who had been condemned and imprisoned.

Abelovsky, the head of the construction division of the Slovak Communist Party, himself came to persuade me to assume the position. He said, if I should run into any trouble with the job, I should just turn to him, and he would fix everything with the authorities. He may have sincerely intended to keep his promise, but when it was called for, he did not back me up.

In general I discovered that at that particular time there were three groups of people around me. The first were those who truly sympathized with me and tried to help me. I could count on their trust, and I place them first, because they were the most important to me, even though they were the fewest in number.

The second group was the most numerous—those who looked upon me as a curiosity. But apart from engaging their passing interest, I meant nothing to them. It made no difference to them what happened to me or how I dealt with the experience. They wanted only to be entertained.

I would have to classify the third group basically as enemies. There were many of them, and they proceeded very deliberately according to a set plan. Their systematic persecution of their opponents was almost scientifically structured. They were not so much concerned about persecuting me and my person as they were in oppressing the church. I was simply a part of the larger target.

In the face of the obvious intentions and encroachment of the state, our church leaders pretended [at the time of this writing] that all was well within the church, and that it had greater prospects and opportunities for progress than it ever had. For this kind of thinking and policy, Bishop General Chabada and others received the Order of Labor from the government.

I say with pain and sorrow that those leaders and others like them never felt the injustices which the church suffered, nor did they really see or understand the injustices, for they never endured them, because they did not live within the church. Their collaboration in the suppression of their own people brought about the disintegration of the SECAV to a degree it had not known previously. As of April 1976 in Slovakia, roughly one-third of the 320 stations of the church were vacant.

That kind of church administration certainly helped fulfill the plans of the atheists to liquidate the church in 20 years. In fact, those church "leaders" became the liquidators—or, as I told Viktor Schimko in 1949, the grave diggers—of the church.

I have documented only a few such cases in this account of mine. Others could well testify to the way this policy affected their lives and ministry for four decades.

Lest I appear to be unduly prejudiced against these people, let me cite some concrete examples.

J. Kmeť had promised that, after my release from prison and following an additional year of "volunteer" brigade service, I could begin my appeal for amnesty and then seek restoration of my preaching license. So, in May 1954, I actually made the appeal for such amnesty and requested a reduction of the five-year loss of civil rights. I submitted my appeal via the district bishop's office in Zvolen.

Bishop Dr. A. L. Katina returned my petition with instructions to reword it, because I was not expressing any regret over my criminal offense. He invited me to Banská Bystrica during the district convention, saying that the district superintendent, Dr. J. V. Ormis, would also be present.

When I appeared there, both of them tried to convince me that without a statement of regret I could not obtain a full amnesty. But I had no idea what kind of criminal offense I was supposed to regret. I reviewed the allegations brought against me and asked them to suggest what I should regret having done for the church. They replied by shrugging their shoulders.

My appeal was sent by the office of the President of the Republic to the Ministry of Justice. The local government officials and I received a reply that my request could not be satisfied, because I had not offered enough evidence of my re-education. Without the restoration of my civil rights, I could not obtain government approval of my reinstatement into the pastoral ministry.

So I continued to work on the construction gang.

31

Partial Restoration at Best

My five-year loss of civil rights finally came to an end May 7, 1958. At once I submitted my request to the bishop general's office for reinstatement into the pastoral ministry. I was thereupon required to complete a biographical resume for the church headquarters. I returned the questionnaire by return mail and waited for a reply.

The recommendation came that I serve a Hungarian congregation in the Levoča region. I declined the offer, because I was not fluent enough in Hungarian to perform my pastoral duties adequately.

In April 1959, Bishop Chabada came personally to the pastoral conference in Lučenec, where we were to agree where I should be placed. As it turned out, he had no time to meet with me during the conference, so we went to the parsonage in Tomašovce, where we were able to confer.

We came to the conclusion that he would get approval for my placement in a vacant parish in Turany. I waited for that approval for a long time. In fact, I am still waiting [17 years later]. And the church did not place me in the pastoral ministry even though, as I mentioned, fully one-third of the stations were vacant.

At the time of my last appeal, the plan to liquidate the church was in full swing. The party functionaries were diligently pursuing it. Consequently a new wave of pastoral trials swept over the church after 1957. The enemies of the church cast their nets, and the "patriotic" clergy exposed pastors and seminarians in order to render them harmless and thereby eliminate them. It will take a long time to ascertain and prove which pastors the church had a hand in arresting, trying, and expelling from pastoral services, and which "pastors" participated in the process.

In the midst of the church's captivity, we could be thankful to God that we could still speak with sincere, caring, and faithful brothers. We could and should thank God for Luther's explanation of the

Fourth Petition of the Lord's Prayer, in which we pray for "good weather, ... good friends, faithful neighbors, and the like."

I thank God also that, even though we have not become cathedrals to his glory, we are at least rocky cliffs of greater or lesser height, against which the destructive avalanche may crash and crumble. I believe the time will come when people will take stones from those cliffs and build temples and cathedrals to the Lord. I believe that the Lord, who is able to raise up children to Abraham from those stones, will create from us and from multitudes of faithful children of God temples of the Holy Spirit and so will establish his kingdom among us in this world. In that kingdom he will bestow his gifts of mercy, love, and peace, gifts spiritual and temporal, so that humanity will not be lacking in anything.

That time is here. Even so, come Lord Jesus!

> [The Lord] said to me, "My grace is sufficient for you, for my power is made perfect in weakness." Therefore I will boast all the more gladly about my weaknesses, so that Christ's power may rest on me.
>
> 2 Corinthians 12:9

151

A Word in Conclusion

Dear Reader,

I have just read this account, as you probably have, in one sitting. To evaluate these memoirs, or to elaborate on my feelings, would interfere with your personal reaction to them. These chapters are written with great clarity and strength. Permit them to affect you, learn from them, be thankful, compare them to your own lifestyle, or criticize them, as you will.

We in Slovakia, as well as in our church, are indebted to such members and to those brothers and sisters of ours who were persecuted more than others during the Communist regime. We need to remember what happened so that those among us who will suffer in the future may not despair that they are surrounded not only by a hostile political system, but by a silent and indifferent church as well.

Brother Pavel Uhorskai never was one who was easily frightened or surrendered to harsh experiences. Unable to re-enter the pastoral ministry after many futile attempts, he spent most of the past two decades [since 1971] serving his home congregation in Tomašovce as a congregational/lay officer and as a cantor at divine services.

Following his release from prison he took an active interest in the life of the church and in theological studies. Officially, the theology of the church conformed to the party line where and whenever necessary. It was impossible and impractical to protest against the prevailing policy publicly. Therefore a group of Lutheran pastors and laymen gathered secretly to analyze the situation biblically and according to the Lutheran Confessions, and circulated their studies by *samizdat* means [i.e., by the underground press] among familiar and trustworthy people. Others in the group to which Brother Uhorskai belonged were Štefan Dlhán, Otto Vizner, Jozef Juráš, Dr. Julius Cibulka, Pavel Hronec, MD Milan Kostra, Eng. Ján Strbka, and others.

After the "revolution" of November 17, 1989, the author met with pastors who were convinced that matters in the church needed to be corrected. For that reason we wanted as a leader of the church an honorable person who had not compromised with the totalitarian system. Brother Pavel Uhorskai was nominated for the office of general bishop and was elected by a large majority of the constituent congregations. He assumed the difficult and responsible role November 1, 1990.

Once again we were able to breathe freely in the church as well as in the state. Even we younger members of the church wondered whether we would live to see freedom restored. Now we see how we would have fared had we not had people who suffered honorably for their convictions. We also had believers, lay and clergy, whom God preserved from imprisonment and cruel suffering, who lived for endless years in tension with the old regime and preserved what they could of the church against unimaginable odds.

Of course, we had our share of "hirelings" also. With deep regret one can trace the influence of politics and totalitarianism on the church and its life. Many of us who wanted parish life to survive could not help but observe the lack of prophetic zeal. There were times when we were afraid to say what we thought. Often silently and with bowed heads we heard radical opinions, and that not only from the mouths of government leaders. Many among us crossed the line of conscience and cooperated zealously with the political system bent on liquidating the church. Now it is from the ranks of those brothers that we are told we should not rummage around in the past and bring to light that which was wrong, but that we should forgive one another and begin to work together in harmony, that only such a policy will help the church to recover.

That is true, but only partially. I do not know of anyone who had much in common with the former regime who has humbly and penitently confessed how it was then, repented, and assured others that he would not do so again. On the contrary, more than one of them considers himself a "martyr" and protector of the church during those difficult times. We are therefore urged to go on without true repentance and without an honorable reconciliation. As we proceed along those lines, we feel that the life of the church is being stifled. Much of what we should have shed we are still dragging along with us.

If, dear reader, you were to ask our brother General Bishop if he is satisfied with everything "as it was" or as it is now, he would no doubt utter a lament similar to the one in his last Christmas pastoral letter in which he deplores the unpleasant relationships between pastors. He bemoans how similar life in our post-communist society, in which we have gotten rid of our common enemy, is to the previous period when we were fighting among ourselves. We have so much to do if we are truly to be "light to the world."

We younger members of the church are trying to understand the overly-sensitive division of people in our older generation, which lived through the Slovak State, World War II, and the confessional struggle between Catholics and Lutherans, as if this were the primary mission of the church. We feel that if we are to live in Slovakia in peace and love, if we are to learn from the past, then this religious division—even if it has to go on forever—must assume a different level of priority among our many spiritual obligations. Over and above our confessional differences, we must believe that as Christians we are children of one heavenly Father. If we fail to learn this, we will not get along even in a democratic society.

We are grateful to God for our honorable sufferers, and for our brother General Bishop. From his memoirs, and from many others now coming to light, we can witness how many Christians of various denominations suffered for Christ. Perhaps the most persecuted among us were the more numerous Roman and Greek Catholics. The record of this suffering ought to be the common precious treasure of Christianity among us. From it we may derive many lessons and many blessings. We must not permit those years and experiences endured by so many anonymously or publicly under the totalitarian communist regime to be wasted or lost by the church under present conditions. Otherwise we will be bringing upon ourselves new punishments and new trials.

I believe that this is what you, dear reader, are also expecting of us. Many of you see our land as your old country, and our church as the community where you or your parents and ancestors first heard the words of eternal life. More than once you have demonstrated your help and love toward us. You are expecting us to work for the good of the church. Our Lord expects that of us even more than you. Obviously we have more opportunities to do so than we have had for the past four decades, and more responsibilities as well.

If you were to ask our brother, Bishop General Uhorskai, what he considers the most important task for today's Slovak Evangelical Church of the Augsburg Confession, he would say without hesitation: missions and evangelism. And this because the church has fallen and needs to be raised to new life. It gladly and zealously assumes this mission, believing that the Lord of the Church who lives, has the power to reawaken even us. "Therefore go and make disciples of all nations ... And surely I am with you always, to the very end of the age" [Matt. 28:19].

Pastor Ján Bohdan Hroboň
Member of the General Council
SECAV

Appendix A

Communication

Ev. A.C. church office, Háj, P.O. Turčianské Teplice

Re: Position statement and comments on the government proposition regarding a change in the relationship between church and state.

Háj, 13 October 1948

To the Secretariat of the Central Action Committee of the SNF, Bratislava

The Secretariat of the Central Action Committee of the Slovak National Front (ÚAV/SNF) has sent to every church office the government proposal for a law concerning the adjustment of salaries, properties, and several other external conditions of the clergy and church, of religious organizations, etc., and indirectly requests pastors to take a personal position toward it and to submit their comments. The Secretariat of the ÚAV/SNF is not following a proper procedure in respect to the Ev. Church of the A. C., whose issues are decided not by individual pastors, but rather in the most democratic manner by all its members. The notice should have been addressed to the entire SECAV, which has already presented the position of all its constituent congregations to the proper office. However, although the Lutheran Pastoral Conference has taken its stand, I herewith present my personal comments and position.

I. General Comments/Reactions

The aforementioned government proposal in essence means the nationalization of the church and its clergy. Heretofore we have witnessed the nationalization of private companies and enterprises which constitute an important value for the state. The church and religion in general are certainly also of inestimable value to the state as well as to all humanity. These fruits do not grow on the tree of the state, but on the tree of life: Jesus Christ; not on the church in union with the state, but from the church in its indissoluble union with Christ, and only as such is the church of infinite importance to the state. The essence of Christianity cannot be valued monetarily by any state, since Christianity is a universal religion.

The nationalization of the church results in a Caesaro-Papism, which has never succeeded anywhere in the past. That is proven most clearly in the state church in Czarist Russia, against which the Soviet Union, immediately after the revolution, took a resolutely exclusory stand and with bitterness of heart remembers it to this day. The sad fate of the Russian (Czarist) state church warns us to beware of a similar step.

The Christian church, and Christianity as such, must not be dependent on pastors either, but only on Christ. How many unworthy clergy were there in the past and are there today? The church has an eternal mission with the eternal Jesus Christ. Take note how many regimes have perished since the appearance of the Christian church! The church, however, did not cause their downfall, even though it was at home in those states, and even though the members of those states were also members of the church.

Nor do we need to go very far from home for examples. Let us look at our own church in the recent past. The national ideologies of the governments under which we lived were so contradictory, that I cannot imagine, nor do I care to think, what would have happened to the church had it been a state church.

The totalitarian Fascist state in Hitler's Germany created its own state church, the so-called "Deutsche Christen," but no Christian, nor even non-Christians, dared to claim that it was Christ's church. The genuine Christians were to be found in the "Confessing Church" (Bekenntniskirche) which was persecuted by the Fascist state. Similarly in the USSR, a state church called the Living Church was formed—and perished. Only the Orthodox church remained independent of the state.

The church grows only where it follows Jesus Christ. Everywhere else it perishes. And only a church founded on Jesus Christ can be of benefit to the state, and to our state, to our beloved Czechoslovak Republic, for which we Lutherans have made so many sacrifices. (See the presentation of President Eduard Beneš to the representatives of SECAV and SEM.)

As is evident from the introduced examples, I foresee a great danger for the church if it were nationalized, i.e., if the proposed

157

motion becomes law. Some dangers will be evident from the following comments on individual paragraphs.

II. Specific Comments/Observations

Par. 1.

Regrettably, this paragraph is concerned only with the material matters of the clergy, whereas it ought to have defined the concept of the clergy. Even until now the state has contributed supplemental support for the clergy, by which it acknowledged the benefits of spiritual workers for the moral and general spiritual nurture of individual citizens, as well as of the state and nation in general. To abolish the individual contributions of church members to their church and for the support of its clergy would limit the members' concern for that which is their most personal possession, worthy of the sacrifice of property and even of life. (Cf., the history of Christian witnesses/martyrs, galley slaves, the Prešov Massacre, etc.)

[To forbid the support of the clergy by their parishioners] would in effect sever the relationship between them in a vital area, to which Marxist materialism precisely attaches such great importance. It would then not be possible to say of pastors that they bear all the sorrows and joys of their members.

Honoraria do indeed have their dark side, especially when they are made as direct payments to the clergy, but the complete removal of honoraria does not assure the elimination of their abuse. That is a matter for the church in arranging its own salary system. Whatever material profit such a clergyman might receive would not harm individual congregations.

Another problem with this paragraph would arise from a claim for equal reimbursement by non-church members and for bona fide members. It is impossible to compensate equally that which is not and that which is.

Par. 2.

Can stand only in the wider interpretation of the passage "and otherwise satisfy the general conditions for the installation of a public employee."

Par. 3.

In general, one cannot object to this paragraph. However, I note, in connection with point 2, that the pastor's overworkload arises not only from the administration of multiple parishes, but also from duties within a single congregation. Playing into this consideration is the number of believers. There is certainly a difference between serving a congregation of 600 members and one numbering 2,000 souls. And even those are not the only figures to be reckoned with. There is the dispersion of the members, the number of preaching stations and scattered members, the distance from the mother church, the number of schools and institutions served, meetings with committees and delegations, etc.

Par. 4–6.

One cannot object to the salary scale except to say that it does not differentiate between large and small congregations, and by barring honoraria from church members, it makes the pastor dependent exclusively upon the state treasury, which can limit his freedom in the performance of his duties, especially in his teaching, preaching, and pastoral activities. In the light of current experience, it is difficult to imagine how the state treasury can manage to survive without new tax levies.

Par. 7.

Independent clergy and deans (seniors) are grouped together in Classification I, with the result that there is no difference in salaries between pastors and supervisors.

Par. 8.

The pension is advantageous for those who retire while this law is in force, whereas it is unfair to those who retired prior to its enactment.

Par. 9.

Honoring the religious instruction in schools of Level I and especially Level II at the same rate is unfair and wrong. The salary scale should be in line with Level III, especially since today the stress is on the middle school and not on the elementary school. Particularly unfair is the payment of two crowns per kilometer of travel. One cannot travel at that rate either by wagon or autobus.

It is also unjust to prescribe that pastors teach religion a certain number of hours, because that is the special function of catechetes, and for ages it was the duty of church school teachers. If a pastor is expected to teach religion classes in school, he should be remunerated accordingly.

Par. 10.

See comments under par. 1.

Par. 11.

For churches this is the most dangerous article. This paragraph is not only superfluous, it is indeed insulting to the church and its autonomous rights. The last sentence especially is offensive: "the government can refuse to grant approval for political reasons."

Thereby the universality of Christianity is in effect buried and replaced by its complete politicization, imposed upon the church by political methods. The church absolutely cannot accept this position. The church is and must remain above political parties in order to be able and allowed to speak Christ's truth to political parties, to the very government itself, to everyone.

I do not know why the ÚAV/SNF did not submit to us Sections II and III of the proposed ordinance. My comments apply to them as well.

Par. 12.

According to this paragraph, the state is in effect taking upon itself the duty of taking care of all the worship expenses of the church, but it alone wants to regulate the level of expenditures. The church would thereby definitely suffer, because it alone best knows what it needs most. If the budget is determined by the state, it could happen that someone who is prejudiced against the church or is totally hostile toward it could regulate the church's budget—which would be disastrous for the very life of the church.

Nor does this paragraph bring any kind of relief for church members. For the profits from all properties and real estate, as well as property rights and the terms of the pastoral call guaranteed by the church—over all of which the state is claiming the right of adjudication—must be counted as the very means of subsistence of the church.

Furthermore, the personal church tax is disproportionately raised to 20 crowns, which is anti-social and unjust. According to the demands of this paragraph, the former budget of my congregation would increase by some 100,000 crowns! Where would these monies come from?

Par. 13.

Is simply the consequence of par. 12.

Par. 14.

Denotes the result of par. 12—the abolition of church autonomy, the surrender of its right to decide its own matters and their place in the context of the church at large.

Par. 15.

The training of pastors depends not only on their material support, but also, and chiefly, on the spirit in which they are administered. This paragraph says nothing whatever of the church's jurisdiction over these institutions, which authority the church cannot surrender when it involves the training of its workers.

Par. 16.

This paragraph abolishes all church treasuries and funds and places them into the hands of the state, irrespective of the wishes and rights of their originators. It impoverishes the receipts from its own source according to par. 13, again to the harm of the church. This paragraph even goes beyond the limits of par. 13.

Par. 17.

This pertains chiefly to the Roman Catholic church.

Par. 18.

This means the total separation of the pastor from the congregation of believers on the financial side, thereby sundering also the spiritual community of believers. (See comments on par. 1)

Par. 19.

This confirms the fact that the church is left with duties, while all rights are assumed by the state.

Par. 20.

See the last paragraph of comments on par. 1. Add one more curious question: Would a society of infidels be placed on the same level as church organizations?

Par. 22.

In order for a law to be consistent, humanly speaking, the voice of the legitimate association of churches, in our case the synods, or the vote of all believers in congregations, must be recognized. This is also the popularly representative, democratic method. Otherwise the church must understand such a law as duress on the part of the state, indeed a definite method of oppression and persecution.

These comments on the proposed law are critical and clearly and overwhelmingly negative. It cannot be otherwise since the church did not request this change, and especially since it had no part in preparing it. I move, therefore, that this proposed law not be enacted, or more accurately, that it not be made into a law, but if there is something in the past situation of the church that needs to be changed—and I can see such a need in our own SECAV, and even more in the Roman Catholic Church—then let it be done by mutual agreement and with respect for the autonomy of the church.

Respectfully,

The Evangelical Church of the Augsburg Confession in Háj

(The seal of the church)

(Signed) Pavel Uhorskai, Ev. A. C. pastor

Appendix B

The Piešťany Manifesto

The Association of Evangelical Pastors in Slovakia [SPEVAK], assembled in Piešťany on September 29, 1949, conferred on the newest proposal of a law regarding state subsidy of the personal and material needs of the church. Based on its sincere and positive loyalty to our Czechoslovak Republic, of which loyalty the highest representatives of our Evangelical Church of the Augsburg Confession [SECAV] have repeatedly assured the honorable President of the Republic and the government, the Association presents its position on the indicated proposal in this Manifesto, which it herewith submits directly to the National Assembly and to the government of the Republic.

MANIFESTO
of the Association of Evangelical Pastors
in Slovakia

Re: the proposed law pertaining to the state subsidization of the personal and material needs of church bodies and congregations.

1. The proposal in question was made without requesting the opinion and cooperation of our Evangelical Church. It is evident also that neither was the opinion of our church sought regarding the first text of this proposed law in 1948.

2. The proposal in no way solves the entire relationship of church and state, because it speaks unilaterally only of subsidizing the material needs of the church, while ignoring the essence and function of the church.

3. The law intends to supply the personal and material needs of the church from the state treasury, thereby fully relieving congregations from contributing to their own needs.

This intention is indeed good from a purely material aspect, but

163

it is based on a total misunderstanding of the church's essence, i.e., that the church is a spiritual community of those who join it voluntarily. For that reason every earthly church should basically be self-supporting, and can at the most accept only a certain amount of support as the state's way to acknowledge the church's important spiritual nurturing which benefits the entire nation. Therefore, church members have both the right and the duty to offer support for the maintenance of the church. The implementation of this right and duty is also a measure of the willingness of church members and an indication of their devotion to the church. Therefore the church may never surrender this willingness and participation of its members.

4. The law wants to make the ordination of pastors and bishops contingent upon the prior approval of government regulation. That would, of course, mean the harsh dissolution of the centuries-old freedom, autonomy, and very dignity of the Evangelical Church. This church has a government-approved constitution, according to which it exercises the ancient right to independently ordain its own pastors and bishops, at every stage of whose administration it is subject only to the Evangelical people's vote in the most democratic manner.

Therefore the Evangelical Church insists by its inherent rights that the state and government, with complete confidence, leave the administration of our church in the hands of the people and duly elected officers of the Evangelical Church, whose pastors and bishops this people calls in a sovereignly democratic manner.

In the proposed establishment of control over the election of pastors and bishops we see an unsubstantiated mistrust of the Evangelical Church, of its members, and of the autonomy of our church, which until now no government regime has disturbed.

5. We have justified fears also that the establishment of the proposed law will lead pastors into a state of legal and social uncertainty, since there are no standards for granting or withholding the state-approved license.

6. The proposal intends to place all the regular needs of the church under state control. This, too, merely gives the appearance of alleviating the financial burden of the church's members, because in reality they will be merely exchanging their support for higher taxes. At the same time, such a regulation destroys the important Biblical

and doctrinal principle that the members of the earthly church have the *duty* as well as the *right* to take care of the material needs of the church and of its workers by themselves. And the same holds true of the church's mission program. If the church's members were not to do this, and the state would do the work for them as a non-ecclesiastical body, they would lose their moral right to call that body their church and would thereby lose their entire basis and reason for taking care of their spiritual and church matters.

Therefore we would see in this law unlimited dangers for the entire church and spiritual life, and so we are opposed to the proposal. Our Evangelical Church has never requested from the state such subsidy for *any* of its economic needs.

7. According to the proposal, all the needs of the church and its congregations, individual and material, its accounts and budgets (i.e., the very means for the performance of its spiritual and mission work) ultimately would be decided by *government* offices. At the same time, the proposal does not even specify *which* [government] offices would have that responsibility.

We consider it basically contradictory, if not absurd, that non-ecclesiastical, non-evangelical, secular agencies should decide church matters and specify the means for carrying out its spiritual program, thereby either favoring or hampering it. Those same people are to make decisions concerning the needs of *all church bodies,* those to which they belong and those to which they do not! This policy would open the doors to the interference of people who have no comprehension whatsoever of the church and spiritual matters and who are in fact totally committed against the church. Doors would be open also to confessional partisanship, jealousy, rivalry, and even injustices, which in turn could considerably upset confessional harmony in communities as well as in higher administrative positions and their operations.

8. The church would be placed under political and police supervision of the state as well as under lower local agencies of control, unlike any other organization founded on the principle of voluntary membership, not even an ordinary recreational organization. The Evangelical Church would have to consider this an expression of unlimited, unsubstantiated, and unjustified distrust—yes, even an insult to itself, to its essence, to its rights and freedoms. This could

have the greatest distressing effect upon the soul of Evangelical people, who have had confidence in their church in times of freedom as well as oppression.

9. The very process of ordaining pastors as well as the material supervision of the church and its congregations would destroy the entire popular democratic principles of our government and the truly democratic supervision and traditions of the Evangelical Church. It would result in tremendous complications, burdens, and bureaucratization while increasing the cost of administering the church's work. In the interest of the work and spirit of the Evangelical Church, and also for financial reasons, we must protest this proposal.

10. Subsidizing all the personal and material needs of the church by the state will mean a new and tremendous burdening of the state treasury—a burden which would increase even more as the work of state agencies, from the ministries down to the local national committees, would multiply greatly, occupied as they would be by immensely superfluous, unnecessary, and harmful details.

11. Our church sees a fatal danger also in this, that if the members of the church no longer contribute directly to the regular needs of their church and their congregations, this could result in a disastrous destruction of a centuries-old order, customs, feelings, and obligations toward the church. The church would be placed in a position where the government could later suddenly remove the church from government protection and discontinue its financial support. In such a sudden separation of the church from the state, the churches would find themselves in a financial crisis, unable to survive. Therefore, this seeming "disburdening" is actually a tearing away of the church from its financial basis. Hence the pastors of the Evangelical Church can never accept this [proposed law] as right and justified, but must consider it an unjustified and unsubstantiated interference detrimental to the Evangelical Church.

12. We look with great fear also on the establishment of the proposal because it places the properties of the Evangelical Church under state control, properties which the Evangelical people voluntarily acquired for their own church. For this reason we think that only the Evangelical people have the right to decide what should be

done with their property, in accordance with the principles of the People's Democracy and the Constitution of our state. We, along with our Evangelical constituency, would have to consider both the limitation of this age-old right [of self-determination over church property] as well as the confiscation of these properties to be painful intrusions into the rights of the people and into the very foundations of the People's Democracy and the will of the people.

13. No matter how the proposal is explained, pastors actually would become officials of the government and would be largely excluded from the rights of the legal church administration. This would make the church, as an organization based on *voluntary* membership, a total absurdity. That method would mean the relapse of the church back into the system of state churches, which in modern states is passé and totally foreign to our Slovak Evangelical people, and would in fact open the doors for the unilateral influence of the predominant denomination or partisan prejudice.

14. The proposal, in par. 17, contains penal sanctions which, in the overall vagueness of the proposal's text and its individual regulations, might trap even the best-intentioned and progressive denominations, congregations, and church officials: penalties and high fines up to 100,000 crowns as well as the loss of freedom up to six months (including imprisonment!)—punishments which could be imposed by the administrative agency itself. Such threats in laws governing the churches would place a truly unbearable pressure on the churches and would make practically impossible the peaceful and free performance of the lofty spiritual, religious, and moral functions of the church. This would also affect our Evangelical Church, which for centuries has made valuable spiritual, national, moral, and cultural contributions to the Slovak people, nurturing in them a humane individual, national, and democratic consciousness. We would consider it to be a most fatal mistake and evil for the nation and state if these contributions were to be hampered in any way.

15. We are convinced that the consistent application of such a law could lead to the dissolution of the historic churches of our nation and at the same time could occasion the rise of various dangerous and fanatical sects, which would pose a definite threat to the church, to the Christian character of our nation, as well as to the nation and state as such.

16. The Association of Evangelical Pastors moves and requests the National Assembly and the government

    a. to remove said proposal of the law from its agenda;

    b. to call a conference of the officials of all church bodies for a free exchange of ideas about the whole issue of the relationship between church and state;

    c. and thus, with a truly mutual understanding, to prepare a law which would clearly resolve all questions of church-state relations on the basis of full equality of the churches, a law which would guarantee the free and peaceful spiritual activity of the church for the spiritual and moral good of its members and for the good of the nation and state.

This Manifesto was prepared with the *unanimous* approval of the Association of Evangelical Pastors in Slovakia in Piešťany, September 28, 1949.

(Signed) Julius Dérer, President

(Signed) Ľudovít Vajdička, Vice-President

(Signed) Štefan Bojnák, Secretary

Appendix C

Profiles of Three Lutheran Martyrs

Otto Vizner

Otto Vizner was condemned in 1962 in a trial of an imaginary group of Lutheran pastors labeled "Čobrda & Company."

Completing his theological studies in Bratislava in the early 1940s, Vizner served as a chaplain in Spišská Nová Ves, Necpaly, and Prešov, and administered congregations in Levoča and Hanušovce nad Teplou. He took part in the Slovak National Uprising [against the Nazis], passed his professorial examinations, and in 1946 became professor/catechete at the *Gymnázium* in Martin.

With the banning of religious instruction in middle schools in 1950, he lost his teaching position and was turned out of his residence at the *Gymnázium*. He served then in Martin as a parish chaplain, but without a permit.

In 1951 he administered a church in the High Tatras. Two years later his government license was revoked. He then went as pastor to Kraskovo, and from there he was transferred to Dačov Lom five years later. It was there that he was arrested in 1962 and tried with the "Čobrda & Company" pastors.

The district court in Banská Bystrica condemned him for subversion of the republic, sentenced him to 14 months' loss of freedom, and an additional sentence prohibiting him from conducting any pastoral activity for five years. Upon an appeal of the prosecution, the supreme court in Prague remanded the case to the district court for rehearing, and he was temporarily set free.

The district court in Banská Bystrica, however, decided to impose the original sentence, a decision confirmed by the supreme court. Otto Vizner was then committed to the prison in Valdice in May 1963 and released conditionally six months later.

The court charged that Vizner's theological writings and translations were politically defamatory, such as the symbolical books, which he discussed with Dr. Čobrda and Struharik, who reviewed the translation. Together with other individuals, he was accused of impeding social progress and influencing youth against Marxist-Leninism.

Prior to his imprisonment, Vizner worked as a trucker's helper in Zvolen. Upon his release from prison he worked as a laborer in a pine forest in Banská Bystrica, then as an officer in a housing construction project, in a central Slovakia poultry farm, in a cooperative market in Zvolen, and from there to retirement in 1981.

Vizner submitted a grievance to the general prosecutor and to the highest court in Bratislava, and requested rehabilitation in 1968, but without success. In 1970 he was given a reduced sentence.

In 1968, Otto Vizner was actively engaged in the renewal movement in the church. He requested restoration of his pastoral license, but was denied. The church refused to assign him to congregational service, would not publish his theological articles and studies in the church periodicals, but on the contrary regarded his interest in church life as subversion of the church.

In spite of persecution, imprisonment, and hard conditions, Otto Vizner worked tirelessly all his life. He wrote several scholarly books, dissertations, numerous studies, articles, essays, and treatises, translated and reviewed many books. Most of his works could not be published. He was an expert theologian, especially in the field of systematic theology, an authority on Luther's writings and current theological trends. He was a sincere believer, a devoted student of God's Word, a zealous worker for the Church and her Lord.

Otto Vizner died in February, 1990, just three months after the restoration of freedom in the country.

Jozef Juráš

Jozef Juráš was one of the most persecuted contemporary Lutheran pastors.

Completing his seminary training in Bratislava, he studied for a year in Erlangen, Germany, until he had to flee under threat from the Gestapo. He returned to Slovakia to serve as a chaplain in Liptovská Porúbka, then as secretary of the Association of Evangelical Youth.

With the Gestapo still on his trail, he escaped from Bratislava to Liptov in 1944, where he joined the preparations for the Slovak

National Uprising. Hiding in the mountains, he organized supplies for the partisans and distributed leaflets. Meanwhile the Gestapo imprisoned his mother and brother.

Upon the approach of the Allied forces, Juráš served as translator and helped organize the supplies of the Czechoslovak and Soviet armies.

After the war, Juráš became the district pastor in Liptovský Mikuláš, in which capacity he established connections with European Lutheran churches, and in 1947 spent half a year studying in the United States. Back home he lectured on his trip. Though gaining favor with his parishioners for his work, he aroused the special watchfulness of government agencies, which threatened him with arrest.

He was duly arrested in 1953, but released without a trial. Immediately after his arrest, his salary was stopped, and his family was left without financial support even during his nine-month hospitalization. His illness was the result of brutal physical abuse during his interrogation, injuries from which he never recovered.

Juráš was arrested while suffering from pleurisy. He was tortured with cold, hunger, beatings, and endless interrogations, during which he was ordered to sign a list of pastors allegedly connected to Western reconnaissance missions, as well as an indictment of the previous church administration for revolutionary activity. He was accused of espionage, treason, sabotage, and insurrection. In the face of brute physical force, he resisted and refused to sign a prepared confession, even after seven months of terrible torture.

From 1954 to 1958 Juráš received government approval to serve a station in Čierna Lehota, and in 1959 he was transferred to Batovce. There he was rearrested in 1962. This time he was accused of being the leader of an imaginary coterie of Lutheran pastors including J. Agneta, Dr. L. Jurkovič, and J. Madarás, and was charged with seditious activity. During his stay in the U. S., he was alleged to have made antigovernment connections and organized subversive activity. During the investigation, Juráš assumed all responsibility in order to divert the attention of the investigators from the other accused Lutheran pastors.

The state court in Košice sentenced Juráš to 13 years loss of freedom and prohibited him for performing any pastoral service for five years. His appeal to the supreme court in Prague was rejected, and he was imprisoned in Valdice, where he gained the highest respect for his behavior even among the jailed Catholic clergy.

As early as 1966, Juráš wrote a letter to Alexander Dubček, but was unable to send it until 1968. In the letter he presented a detailed and accurate analysis of the post-February development of the church, and described the details of his own case. Neither in Juráš's case, nor in the judicial processes of other Lutheran pastors, do we find any compromise of Christianity with Marxist materialism. The party and government agencies opposed the adherents of Christianity not on the ideological level, but with crude force and falsehood.

Jozef Juráš had to wait until 1968 to be released from prison by federal amnesty. After his release he spent four months in the hospital. In a rehabilitation hearing in Košice, he was declared not guilty, but the supreme court in Bratislava, at the complaint of the prosecutor, reversed the rehabilitation decision in 1970. So Juráš never did get to receive his rehabilitation.

Broken in health, Juráš organized a congregation in Bratislava–Petržalka and served it from 1969 to 1972. When he reached the age of sixty, his license was revoked, and he was forced to retire.

Thereupon he worked as a proofreader, and spent the last year of his life in a hospital, where he succumbed to the results of heavy torture in 1975. Neither his death nor his funeral was publicized, and the choir he had trained was not permitted to enter the cemetery.

Dr. Julius Cibulka

Among the most prominent Lutheran pastors to suffer persecution was Dr. Julius Cibulka.

Completing his theological studies in Bratislava, Cibulka studied for a year in Strasbourg, France. He returned to serve as congregational chaplain in Trenčín, then as pastor briefly in Malé Stankovce, and from 1932 in the Myjava church. Those were years of blessed ministry as preacher, pastor, evangelist, editor, administrator, and cultural enlightener. Simultaneously, Cibulka was expanding his theological knowledge. He obtained a doctorate in theology while majoring in philosophy and sociology at Comenius University.

Publicly, Dr. Cibulka acquired a reputation as a zealous pastor, educated scholar, dedicated worker, and as a person capable of holding the highest position in the church. Politically, he also joined the Czechoslovak resistance to Fascism.

In 1947, Cibulka continued his successful work in Bratislava, where he inspired youth by his example and impressed the intellectuals and common folk with his leadership qualities. As he became a leading figure in the Bratislava congregation and in the community, he aroused the opposition of the church's new leadership.

He did not join ÚSEK (the Coalition of Slovak Evangelical Pastors), comparable to the Catholic Pacem in Terris, created to replace the disbanded SPEVAK (the Association of Evangelical Pastors in SECAV). As a result he had to leave Bratislava under the conditions of Action B, was deprived of his state license, and transferred to the parish in Háj in 1951.

It was in that same year that Pastor Pavel Uhorskai was arrested in Háj. The congregation defended its falsely accused pastor and worked for his release. It sought in vain for assistance from then General Bishop Chabada. As a consequence of its action, the congregation came into disfavor with state authorities and the situation in the parish deteriorated greatly. Dr. Cibulka, however, won the support of the congregation with his sensitive approach while under the constant scrutiny of political and church agencies.

Increasingly he became the object of conjectures and criticisms, with the result that his preaching license was revoked in 1966, and he was given a small congregation in Limbach among expatriated Germans. The town's inhabitants were gathered from all parts of Slovakia, and the congregation was in poor condition. However, with typical zeal and patient work, Dr. Cibulka revitalized this congregation also.

Cibulka took an active part in the church renewal movement in 1968–69. As he himself admitted, he was concerned "about the revival of our church, torn and dirtied by the darkness of a long night and its degrading service of the will and power of the world, and chained by a rude and lawless supervision of its pastors and members."

In May 1968, Dr. Cibulka helped organize a conference of Lutheran pastors in Turčianské Teplice, where he presented a paper on "The Spiritual Renewal of the Church." The administration of the church nominally participated in the movement for a while, but soon reverted to its policy of deformation and injustice, revealing its underlying interest in power. Dr. Cibulka described the course of the renewal movement in *The Deceptive Daybreak*.

This brief period was followed by investigations and ploys by church and state to implicate Cibulka in dissenting activity. His state permit was revoked from his pastorate in Limbach, and he was forced to retire in 1972. For five years thereafter he worked in the city museum.

Dr. Julius Cibulka died in 1985. His funeral was not permitted to be held in the church where he had preached for many years.

Appendix D

Studies by Pavel Uhorskai

1941: *Church History in Slovak Literature* (40 pp.)

1942: *Bibliography for Lutheran Youth* (catalog) (12 pp.)

1942: *The Worship of God in Lutheran and Catholic Theology* (25 pp.)

1942: *The Head of the Church in Catholic and Lutheran Doctrine* (45 pp.)

1943: *Politics in Christianity* (30 pp.)

1943: *The Church and the Kingdom of God* (50 pp.)

Note: All these works were confiscated by the State Security Police (ŠTB) when General Bishop Uhorskai was arrested, and they were subsequently burned, together with all materials related to youth ministry and all sermons written during the nine-year activity of Pastor Uhorskai.